ELEVATE
Self Awareness through Courage, Potential, and Fulfillment

Dr. Keppen Laszlo

Elevate

Elevate— Self Awareness through Courage, Potential, and Fulfillment

Copyright © 2014 by Dr. Keppen Laszlo

ISBN: 978-1495290398

Book interior design by Abigail Beers

http://www.upwork.com/o/profiles/users/_~010b638a876dba95bb/

Cover Design by The Solution Machine

Cover pictures by Dawn Leget

dawnlegetphotography.com

Dedication

This book is dedicated to my family and friends. Jen, my beautiful wife, your support through all of my career victories and challenges have given me such strength to get done what I need to get done. Your love and support for me and our family is unprecedented. Thank you. Thank you. Thank you.

To my two boys, Jay and Karson, you were my inspiration to write this book. May these thoughts permeate your souls and know that this book is what and who we are. May you take these words and grow upon them yourselves so that someday when you are ready to shine your light, you will be equipped to do so.

Mom, thank you for pouring your love and belief into me as a child. You set the foundation to help me believe that I can achieve anything I set my mind to.

Pops, although you are gone now, your mentorship and stability gave me hope at such a crucial time in my life. Thanks for teaching me to always have a goal.

Uncle Lazz, you put the first self-development books in my hands and for that I will always be grateful. Thank you for investing your time and energy in me and always reminding me that success is attainable, and that it is a choice.

Thank you to my team at Discover Health and Wellness. Your involvement and excitement on this project really propelled me when I needed it.

Lastly, to my best friends, thank you all for giving me inspiration to make a difference and to truly *Elevate* our world.

Elevate

Contents

Introduction

It is going to be an honor to serve you over the next several chapters. I truly feel this book will set you on a path that will allow you to obtain everything you want and desire. It is meant to develop you as a person, inside and out, for the better. This book is meant to meet you where you're at in your life's path. You and I are about to go on a journey you will never forget, my friend.

When I originally had the idea for this book, it was going to be for parents. I have two unbelievably inspiring boys, and I wanted this book to be a Dad's lessons to his kids. As the concept of this book began to take place in my mind, I realized it was a book for people who want to achieve greatness *and* who want to make a difference. It was written for people who desire to get crystal clear on: who they are, why they are here, what they want, how they are going to get it and how their contributions to this world will make it a better place. It is a book for leaders—the masters and the students.

Our country needs people that not only want the best for themselves, but who also want the best for others. This book is a movement. It seems like every month, if not every week, there is another terrible tragedy happening to our society. Recently, our country experienced another school shooting. Many solutions have been discussed, such as locking down our schools and adding surveillance systems and armed security. This may help to an extent; however, the fundamental solution is to start with ourselves. You may have heard the famous Gandhi quote, "You must be the change you wish to see in the world." This book is about how I believe we can do that.

As far as the book's style and theme, I deliberately go back and forth between first and third person, based on the principle I am writing on, to deliver the point. I use "he" most of the time to avoid going back and forth between he and she. When I use a masculine pronoun such as "he," it is referring to both the male and female person, both *he* and *she. This book is a relaxed conversational type of read.* Imagine you and I, knee to knee, or shoulder to shoulder, as the words begin to take seed in your mind and heart. Some language may be strong and some content may be offensive. This is meant to wake you up, to feel the rain, to not just get wet. Some sections will resonate with you and some may not. Some sections may be very familiar to you and some may blow your mind. Commit to the process of completing it. Read it without judgment, and if anything, read it to gain a different perspective on life. The chapters are concise, with bottom line topics, designed to be read from front to back. However, if you want to bounce around chapters in the book, you can certainly do that.

I have affirmations and quotes throughout the book in which I have collected for over twenty years. I have done my best to give proper credit. If I was unable to find the quote through a search, I gave credit to the first person I heard it from. If I was unable to recall whom I heard or read it from, I did not reference it directly. In the acknowledgment section of this book, I have listed every mentor and teacher that has influenced my life in a positive way. This is my way to give credit to all who have gone before me.

In the conclusion of the book, I have listed Chapters and the coinciding practical applications. I believe these pillars are the fundamentals of achieving what you want. The practical applications in the conclusion section are what will take you from knowledge to results. Read the book in its entirety and *then* begin the practical applications. If you are anything like me, I have read some books that have me do a practical at the end of each chapter, and I either skip it or don't pick the book up until I create the time to perform the practical. I don't prefer that. I have found that reading the book in its entirety, making the highlights, and then bringing the action in at the conclusion is what works best.

Our website, www.ElevateBook.com/Bonus, has videos correlating to each chapter. Watch the videos after each chapter or watch them at the end of the book. You can also get a free *Elevate* affirmations poster there as well as your *Elevate* Score. You can see where you rank before you start the book.

I believe we should only take advice from people we want to be like. I certainly don't believe I have it all figured out, and I will always live my life as a lifetime learner. Sometimes I get it right, and other times I totally blow it. So why should you listen to me? That is a great question. Bottom line, knowledge is results, not intellect. I am about to gloat a little bit, simply for the purpose of establishing credibility. This is not my style; however, I want you to feel confident that these pages come from a man that has done fairly well in many areas of his life. I write from experience and I hope to get even more of it as I continue to grow and develop as a human being.

So here are a few of the things I have been proud of.

Remember, in listing some of my achievements, they are simply here to inspire you to achieve what is important to *you*. As you read more of the book, you will see that no matter where you are starting from, you *can* achieve greatness.

Before age thirty-five, I had built and sold my first business, and before turning forty, I owned and operated one of the largest chains of health and wellness centers in my state. Some of my personal accomplishments that I am proud of include qualifying and competing in the Junior Olympics and earning my first degree black belt; graduating in the top ten percent of my class with honors and earning my Doctor of Chiropractic degree at age twenty-four; and achieving first place in a Toastmasters contest for the district.

I began a personal relationship with God over twenty-five years ago and have been an avid student of self-growth for over twenty years now. I have studied abroad in Guadalajara and have traveled to many countries around the world. I have a *wonderful* family and a *wonderful* marriage that is going on twelve years. Finally, I ran my first marathon last year. Whew! If I can become the type of person that goes after what they want, then so can you! So, let's humbly go down this path of life together, shall we? After you.

Elevate

Part One
The *Elevate* Self: Your Beginning to Greatness

Elevate

1Chapter One:
Love

"Today is a day filled with love, opportunity, and potential."

-Marshall Sylver

It's time to love. I know this sounds sappy or cliché, but it's true. It's time to love God, love ourselves, and love people. First of all, I just used the word God. Either you are drawn toward the word God, or you are repelled by the word God. There was a time in my life when I cringed at the very mention of God. Thankfully, that was over twenty years ago. Let me clear up some things, because God is referenced throughout this book. My job is not to teach religion or save your soul. My job is to speak fundamental truths and bring them into your life so you can achieve what you want. Part of those fundamental beliefs is that you are God's creation. You and I both know that much turmoil has been experienced regarding the subject.

This book assumes that we can all move forward knowing that God is the source of life. He has many different names and is experienced in many different ways. When I reference God, I am referring to the source of our existence, our creator, our purest example of love. If you don't believe in a creator, then continue reading anyway. If you do believe in a creator but do not believe He is a loving one, then continue reading anyway. This book is about a movement, so even if you are an atheist, you can still get behind what I am proposing the love of God represents. It's good stuff! Fair? Okay.

So what is love? Love is unconditional acceptance of ourselves and of others. I believe a huge aspect of love, and especially unconditional love, is simply the act of understanding where others are coming from. For example, hurt people in our society hurt other people. I do believe there are consequences to our actions, regardless of why we did them. However, if we can see that the people who perform harmful, destructive acts toward others are hurt themselves, it helps our ability to get on board with the concept of love. If we can practice unconditional love toward ourselves and others, then others see our example and the results this action portrays in our lives. If others can see this in us, they will want what we have, and we can influence others for the better.

I ran into a checkout clerk the other day who was clearly having a really, really bad day. She was rude and upset. My first instinct was to treat her the way she was treating me; however, I remembered that people need love the most when they deserve it the least. Her bad attitude was really disguised as a plea for someone to love her. I softened my voice, looked her in the eyes with a compassionate look on my face and sincerely said, "One of those days, huh?" She literally started to cry. This simple connection with another human being made her cry. All I did was relate to her and let her know with five little words that it was going to be okay. We all have bad days now and then. She was smiling by the time our brief interaction was over, and I like to think that she was much more pleasant with the customers next in line.

When we are the change, others become the change, and slowly, we get back to a society that cares for each other. Slowly, we get back to a society that loves one another. Slowly, we get back to a society where we don't have to be as concerned about the next bombing or tragedy. I know this is a lofty aspiration, but hey, let's be the change and go from there.

A mom of one of our long-time wellness patients called me the other day from the hospital, letting me know that her teenage daughter was threatening suicide and had been admitted. Nearly forty thousand people take their own lives a year in the US alone.[1] When the word suicide came up, I knew it was absolutely time to show love in action. What was surprising to me was that this was the same girl that came in to our wellness center years ago in a wheelchair, paralyzed from the waist down. A year earlier she had received a vaccination and had an "allergic reaction," which paralyzed her from the waist down. She was told there was nothing she could do and was bound to a wheelchair for the rest of her life. Prior to this experience, she was an active cheerleader, chasing her dreams.

She was referred to our office and we got to work. With a combination of chiropractic, physical therapy, massage, and toxicity cleanses, she not only got out of her wheelchair, but she is now doing back handsprings on the cheerleading squad! Her paralysis is gone! It was a miracle, for sure. She had no hope, was told that there was no hope, and then she was led to some people that gave her a chance, that gave her love. Miracles still happen, folks. It starts with you.

So, getting back to her currently, why in the world would she consider suicide after such a miraculous second shot at life? Well, long story short, her boyfriend broke up with her. I sat next to her and her mom, knee to knee, and let her know over and over again that she was made for a purpose. God loves her and has a plan for her life. She is destined for greatness. She may have a variety of heartbreaks in her life, but they will always make her stronger. I told her that she is special and that so many people love her. I told her there are many people needing her help and that she needed to be strong in order to be such a wonderful inspiration for others. As tears began to flow, I knew I had delivered another human being love, unconditionally, no judgment, no strings attached, just pure love. By the end of our visit, she told me that her experience with our offices has inspired her to become a physical therapist, and I believe she will. She was again focused on the gifts of life and her future.

So how do we love God, ourselves, and people? Let's start with God. How do we love God? How do we love our Creator? How do we understand that this is where internal joy comes from? Start by waking up every morning in a state of gratefulness. Be grateful for the power of life. Affirm to yourself, "Thank you, God, for this day. Thank you for everything in my life. I was created to shine; thank you." There is only one you, and you were beautifully and wonderfully made. There's a plan for your life. Continue to develop a relationship with God and believe deep down to your soul that you were made for a reason. You'll develop a sense of peace and understanding that surpasses everything. If you haven't told God how thankful you are, give it a shot. If you already do this, do it more often. When we know we are loved and that God is looking out for us, and we know that we have a fabulous future ahead of us, we become grateful. It permeates our soul, our entire being. People around you will notice that there is something special and uniquely different about you when this mentality becomes part of you. God represents: Unconditional Love, Strength, Wisdom, Encouragement, Security, Guidance, Peace, and Understanding. The more you love God, the more of these qualities you experience.

When we know we are loved and that God is looking out for us, and we know that we have a fabulous future ahead of us, we become grateful.

Even atheists can get behind this movement by practicing what God represents. It's true. If it makes it easier, replace the word God with the word Life. Regardless of what you believe, practice these qualities and your love will shine. I know that the word God represents different things to different people. I know that for some, the word represents an angry judgmental God with lightning bolts, sending people to eternal damnation with lakes of fire. Well, how is that working for you? If that view is what is keeping you from loving a creator then do you think it might be time to look at a different view? I hope so.

My team of wellness doctors takes the power of unconditional love very seriously. Love heals. It is the answer. Once, recently, we were downtown, passing out flowers to people we thought could use a small gesture of love. We would hand them a flower and say to them, "You matter and I love you as a person." It was a small gesture that made a big impact. I saw one of our doctors getting lectured at pretty sternly by a preacher with a megaphone in one hand and a Bible in the other. Next to him was a huge sign that said LOVE. My doctor friend originally went over to him to give him a flower and tell him how awesome it was that he was out there spreading love, too. You might have an idea where this is headed.

As he was getting lectured, I walked over and the preacher asked what church we were with. We told him we were not with a church; we were here for a movement. We told him we were giving people flowers as a sign of unconditional love and acceptance of one another. He then told us we were spreading hate, not love, and by not telling them about the gospel we weren't helping mankind. We told him we were not out there for religion, that we were out there to show others kindness. He wasn't having it and continued to lay into both of us. It was time to walk.

I told the preacher that I loved him for being convicted to speak his truth. And I sincerely meant it. It is hard to stand up for what you believe in. As we walked away, he then got on his megaphone and shouted, "These two guys with the flowers are not spreading love, they are spreading hate. They are not saved. They are the antichrist!" Yes, he really called us the antichrist. Didn't Christ himself spread the message of unconditional love and acceptance? Well, okay, moving on, I understand why many have a problem with the term "God", and for the record, this type of preacher represents a very, very small percentage of men and women that have dedicated their lives to leading and teaching people about a loving God. So, step one is to love God. Practice what God represents. See yourself begin to shine.

Next, love yourself. The key to loving yourself is to know that God made you incredibly unique, special, beautiful, and for a purpose. You are here for a reason. You were given unique gifts and talents that were meant to help you feel alive and vibrant. Later, we will explore your gifts and talents and how you can share those gifts and talents with the world. This is the beginning to loving yourself. I know for some, they can get behind the idea of a creator, but not one that loves us and thinks we are unique, special, beautiful, and gifted. After all, how can a loving

God allow so many bad things to happen to good people, right? I dive into this subject in great detail in the Faith and Spirituality chapter. I dive into it because the questions I attempt to answer there have troubled me my entire life. So if you fall into the skeptic category, I am asking you to abandon all of that and for now, focus on practicing unconditional love toward yourself. Fair? Okay.

When you know you were made for a purpose, and when you do what you were made to do, you will be shining so much that you can't help but love yourself. This is the ultimate result in your life showing that, yes, you love yourself enough to do what you were meant to do. There are many other factors in loving yourself which we will explore. For now, know that you were made for a purpose. Begin to really feel that and watch love emanate. Your future is so bright you're going to need sunglasses!

Lastly, love people. One way to do this is to help others. Contribute. I don't believe we were born to keep our talents to ourselves. I believe we have a moral right to help others and bring them closer to their purpose, to give them opportunities to elevate themselves. Don't you feel great when you are helping someone with your time or money? Have you done that lately? Who needs help around you? Who do you know that truly wants to better themselves? Help someone today, small or big, give it a shot. Help others. This is the ultimate action step in loving people.

In summary, we have discussed *loving God, loving ourselves*, and *loving people*. Let's be that change to ourselves so we can see that change in the world. Start with yourself, let it shine to the people closest to you, and let that cycle continue until we see a positive change.

> **Bottom line:** The best gift you can give yourself is the gift of God's love. When you are loved by a source greater than man, it gives you the strength and power to love yourself. When you love yourself, it gives you the strength and power to shine that love to others.

Elevate

2Chapter Two: Character

"If you don't stand for something,
you will fall for everything."
-General George S. Patton

Character is still relevant, right? With the prevalence of the "in it to win it" mindsets these days, character seems to be an old-fashion term for some of us. However, for most of us, it still carries great significance. I want to explore what character is, why it is so important to be happy, and how character helps us get what we want.

So what is character? Character is the sum of all of your virtues. It affects every single area of your life. When you build your character, it gives you vitality. When you destroy your character, it eventually destroys you. Based on the daily decisions you make, character can be slowly whittled away or slowly built to greatness. It must be continually developed and guarded daily.

I live in beautiful Colorado, and we get to experience seasons here. Last fall, this huge oak tree caught my attention. All of its leaves had fallen, and I was able to see its gigantic core and many branches. It inspired me to contemplate on character. Character is like that mighty oak tree. The strong core in the middle represents our core values. It represents who we are and what we stand for. It represents our vision and our purpose. The harder and longer we work on our character, the deeper our roots become and the thicker our core gets. The more resistance we take against our core and the more decisions we make that we know are the right ones, the stronger that core becomes. As we grow this foundation, our life begins to branch out into what become the key areas of our life.

The branches represent what is most important to us. Every decision we contemplate runs through those branches and then to the core, our character. When we make the right decisions, decisions that come up every day in those key areas of our life, the core and the branches get bigger and stronger until eventually, we stand as that mighty oak does. Even if we currently feel that our core is weak, and it could be taken out by a small gust of wind, we know we have the choice to build from there and become that mighty oak. And hey, if it makes you feel better, know that even the mighty oak started out as a little nut.

YOUR VIRTUES IN ACTION

"My momma always said...," okay, really now, my mom always told me that I was only as good as my word. My grandfather spoke these words of wisdom to her and she passed them on to me. This phrase served me very well. It became one of my highest virtues. People who know me know that I do what I say I am going to do. I don't always get it right, but this has certainly been a great virtue for me to live by.

So how is your character? Let's do a check in. What are the key virtues that you live by? For example: Honesty, Respect, Loyalty, Faith, Courage, Love. Let's call these the Big Six. What are they for you? Deliberately following your virtues is your key to emotional freedom.

Let's look at these virtues in action.

Honesty:

Tell the truth, folks. Be honest with yourself and others. People deserve it. Now, if honesty becomes cruelty, then don't say it! Watch what you say. It is more important to be kind in some situations than *brutally* honest. Soften your words; be kind.

Respect:

Most of us know the golden rule: Whoever has the most gold makes the rules. Just kidding, although that is very true. I am referring to a different golden rule. Heck, if we want, we can go golden *or* platinum. The golden rule: Treat others as you want to be treated. The platinum rule: Treat others the way they like to be treated. Both rules are great. Just respect each other. When you have respect for yourself, you will have respect for others.

One way to show respect is while you are driving. One morning, I accidentally cut someone off and they promptly put their finger out the window and showed me I was number one. I got the one finger salute! All I could think of was how miserable that person must be. It was unfortunate that my little mistake put them in such a huge reckless state. I felt sorry for them. Here's a great rule to follow: When I am angry, I am stupid. Respect each other and don't let others who disrespect you pull you into anger.

Loyalty:

I am referring to honoring your commitments here. Loyalty is when you do what you say you are going to do. If we don't deliver on what we said we were going to do, it causes a small piece of mistrust to build up in others toward us. Eventually, when someone knows they can't count on you, well, that is pretty much the beginning of the end. If you say you are going to do it, then do it. If you don't do it, apologize and make it right. Loyalty is about keeping your commitments to yourself and to each other.

Faith:

Trust that God has destined you for greatness. Expect the best out of life. Trust that everything is going to be okay. Trust that whatever is happening at the time, whether good or bad, will somehow serve you for the better in the long run. We all have faith, even if we don't think we do. Every time you kiss your family goodbye for the day, you are practicing faith that everyone will return home safely.

Courage:

To be able to say, "I love you" to those you don't like or to those you don't know is the highest form of self-growth there is.

Courage is going after what you want. Courage is stepping up to fear and pushing through it. Courage is going after what you want despite the voice inside telling you not to. We go into this one deeper later on.

Love:

Looking beyond our own various self-interests and performing actions that benefit others is the highest form of character in action. Isn't unconditional love the ultimate in achieving bliss? To be able to say, "I love you" to those you like is remarkable. To be able to say, "I love you" to those you don't like or to those you don't know is the highest form of self-growth there is.

CONGRUENCY

So what virtues do you want to live by? Do the ones above resonate? While defining what virtues you would like to live by, one tool is to recognize if you are performing any actions that aren't congruent with who you are.

For example, is there conflict between who you are personally and professionally? Recently our company, Discover Health and Wellness, updated our personnel handbook, and the topic of social media came up. We employ professionals that are credible leaders to our patients, and it is important to us to respect that image. We had an experience where one of our team member's personal Facebook page wasn't, well, let's just say, professional, and some patients were *friending* the team member. It brought up multiple discussions regarding who we are in the office and who we are outside of the office and how that relates to our brand. We debated whether policy should be created requiring team members to have a personal and a professional Facebook page, because our patients can easily look up the team members if they want to. We decided against it and let the team members know that who they are outside of the office needs to reflect who they are inside of the office. Would you be okay with your boss visiting your Facebook page?

How about having different groups of friends? Do you have work friends, church friends, and/or party friends? Would you not want to be around all of your groups of friends at the same time? Would it make you feel uncomfortable if one friend wanted you to chug a beer bong and go to the strip bar in front of the other friend that was a person of influence in your company or church? You get the point. If you have two different lives, continue to look at that and see where they are not congruent. You deserve congruency for your own wellbeing. Be yourself in all situations. Be yourself and be okay with yourself regardless of where you are at or who you are with.

So what are your key virtues? Take this as a challenge. We are all works in progress. Which virtue of character do you need to work on? Give yourself a ranking of one to ten, with ten being the best. How would you rank yourself in the Big Six: Honesty, Respect, Loyalty, Faith, Courage, and Love? Pick the one with the lowest score and get to work! Your life is worth it.

I was having lunch with a friend of mine last week, and we were talking about homelessness. He had just come from volunteering, and he said they had handed out lunches to about two hundred homeless people. We both have different views on this; however, we can definitely see each other's points. I will jump into this in a later chapter. After lunch,

I was walking back to the office, and I came upon this young man in his late teens, early twenties. He was on his phone, pants down to the middle of his butt and his hat on crooked. I judged him. I did. I failed my little character test for the day. Damn, I'm still a work in progress!

So as I passed him, he asked if I had a dollar. We continued to walk side by side, and I said, "Yes I do. I have lots of dollars." I kept walking and he was keeping up with my pace. There was an awkward silence and he said, "Well, can I have one?" I looked at him sincerely and said, "Why should I give you a dollar?" He said it was for a meal. I told him, "Look, I was poor for a long time, and I have had to make really good choices and much sacrifice to get where I'm at today. Do you have a job?" Something clicked in him and he began to get very passionate about the fact that, although he did not have a job, he had a purpose. He told me about how he writes lyrics for the youth to encourage them to do good in the world and make a difference. I told him I was not going to give him a dollar, but that he could walk with me if he still wanted to. He did. I told him about the *Elevate* movement, the book I was writing, and how our purposes line up. We introduced ourselves to each other, and, with a huge smile, he said his friends call him "Sweets." We laughed together.

He gave me his number, and I told him I might call him to shoot some hip-hop videos on our site, www.ElevateBook.com/Bonus. He said that he hopes that I do. For the record, I did. Check out the video. After our walk, I gave him ten bucks and said, "You don't sound like someone who should be asking for money; go get some lunch."

HAPPINESS THROUGH CHARACTER

How is the reputation you have with yourself? I know this can be a tough question. The biggest slap in the face that you can ever experience is thinking that you are "the only one that will know." A huge part of your happiness is how well you are following your virtues. Following your virtues makes you feel better about yourself, especially in a society today where it is becoming harder to find good virtues. No one is perfect. If you cross your virtues, then stop, reset, and carry on.

If you feel that empty gloom inside, it's time to visit your character. If you feel that this is all there is, then it's time to get yourself back on track. Bottom line, character is your integrity gauge. The law of integrity is when what you say, think, and do is consistent. Folks, practice this law of integrity and get ready to unleash the fury of high self-esteem. A high self-esteem will bring all sorts of joy into your life. When you treat others how you would want to be treated yourself, your self-esteem rises. When your thoughts match what you say, and when what you say matches what you do, you enter the highest state of integrity.

Contradiction is self-destruction. Solid integrity is about consistently making decisions that are congruent with who you are. It takes courage to live an integrity-filled life. The word *integrity* literally is defined as one hundred percent whole. Live with integrity or choose to live with the feeling of knowing that you consistently and deliberately make the wrong choices. That doesn't work! The more you practice integrity, the higher your self-esteem rises, and the more you will feel better about yourself. You will be more fulfilled emotionally, make more money, have more solid loving relationships, and have the ability to conquer more fear on a regular basis. When you feel better about yourself, it affects everything that is important in your life. Do you know what the difference is between self worth and self esteem? You are born with one hundred percent self worth, however self esteem is earned.

> **Bottom line:** If you know what virtues you live by and deliberately live your life by them, you will be right with yourself. Your character will be solid, and you will become a person of great influence, giving you the ability to help others and yourself succeed.

3 Chapter Three: Moral Code

"I'd rather have the whole world against me than my own soul."

-Dr. John Demartini

Before we open up this chapter, it is important to note why it is part of the ultimate life success formula. Here's the answer. Once we can define our morals with clear certainty, we embrace a newfound confidence that makes us happier and more successful to complete what we need to complete to make things happen. I have found that there is great confusion regarding morals in our society, and I hope to deliver a point of view and put forth questions that may provide an answer.

WHAT IS MORAL CODE?

Socrates defined moral code as "how we ought to live." Moral code is a group of standards, laws, or rules within a group or society. Once we establish what our moral code is, we can then recognize when we don't follow it. Once we recognize it, we have the opportunity to correct it.

Most religious books, for example, contain moral code. The challenge is defining what group of moral codes and standards we can all agree on and follow. In general, we should use self-responsibility for our choices and actions and respect the rights of others. It has been my experience that rules are there to protect us, and when agreed on by the majority, they should be followed in order to remain a cohesive society. When they are not, we have anarchy. A society with anarchy is like watching a basketball game where there are no rules. It just doesn't work. At the same time, some rules of our society may not line up with our morals or equal rights of all and need to be liberated. For example, burning witches at the stake or extinguishing a race based on law would not be following moral code, regardless of what the law says about it. Life, and rules in general, are not always as clear as black and white.

WHAT IS SIN?

The word *sin* stirs up quite a bit of emotion for some people. It is usually because the word invites us to look at what we are not doing right in our lives and how it is affecting us. If you have an emotional charge to the word, maybe I can help. There is very much a right and wrong. Unless you are a sociopath, and lack sympathy or remorse, then you have a moral code. That little voice inside will be your guidance.

When you perform an act against your own moral code it lowers your self-esteem and eventually causes you to be critical toward yourself and others if not corrected. When continued and not put in check, it leads to a miserable life. When I meet someone who is bitter, quick to anger, and apathetic, it is obvious they have not confronted an area of their life that is causing these non-serving emotions. If you fall in this category, it is a huge clue to look at where you are breaking your moral code. It's time to check it before you wreck it. It's time to move forward, right?

When we "sin" it is another way to say we are getting off track. The original biblical Hebrew root of the word sin means to "miss a target" or to "have an error." There is a plan for your life. Your job is to stay on track and not miss the target. It's like a vehicle navigation system. I put in where I want to go, and if I get off path, it lets me know and reroutes me to get back on. When we sin, it gets us off track. Let's look at what right and wrong is in the first place.

RIGHT AND WRONG VERSUS GOOD AND BAD

Have you ever heard the Shakespeare quote from Hamlet, "There is nothing either good or bad, but thinking makes it so"? I have seen people take this quote literally and use it as an excuse to basically ignore right and wrong. This is ludicrous. It is the same type of thinking that says, "I know what I am about to do is wrong, but I will just ask for forgiveness later." This level of thinking completely ignores character. It keeps us in a state of non-congruency. For example, just because something feels right does not always make it right. Just because something can be forgiven later, does not make it okay. There is very much a right and wrong, and although entire books and debates have been written and discussed from the age of man on the topic of ethics, fundamentally, we all have that voice inside that is our guidance of right and wrong.

It is important, therefore, to understand the difference between right and wrong versus good and bad. They are not the same. Right is not synonymous with good, and wrong is not synonymous with bad. Here is a clear distinction. Right and wrong refer to our moral code or our personal ethics. Good and bad refer to how we *interpret* actions or situations. These are two totally different concepts. The difference is, right and wrong is an action, and good and bad is an *interpretation* of the action.

The Shakespeare quote makes much more sense when we interpret the words good or bad correctly and not confuse those with right or wrong. Shakespeare was correct when he said it is how we think about good and bad that makes it so. Once again, this is referring to situations. Remember, good and bad is our interpretation.

How we interpret situations is what will make it good or bad in our minds. For example, if a hurricane wiped out forty thousand people, that was not right or wrong. We had no control over that action. However, we do have control over the choice on how we *interpret* the hurricane that killed forty thousand people. That will make it good or bad to us.

> *How we interpret situations is what will make it good or bad in our minds.*

How about the man that has newfound wealth? At first he interpreted it as good, and yet, he had a weak character and began doing drugs because of his extra money and became addicted to cocaine and lost everything. Was the newfound wealth a good or bad thing? You tell me.

Here's a story to illustrate the point. A wise man won the lottery many years ago. His friends and family celebrated with him and said, "That is fantastic! This is so good." The wise man smiled and said, "I don't know about that." He enjoyed his wealth for many years. He helped many people, traveled the world, and bought everything he ever wanted, including a big, beautiful home. He even bought a brand new helicopter. One day he crashed his helicopter due to a mechanical failure and nearly died. He ended up puncturing his lung and breaking his back. His family and friends visited him in the hospital and said, "This is so bad, you poor thing! How terrible this is." The man said, "I don't know about that." While he was in the hospital, in the middle of the night, his beautiful home burned to the ground from an inescapable forest fire. His friends and family said, "Oh, thank God you were here in the hospital last night!" The man replied, "I don't know about that." And so the story goes.

Where confusion on ethics happens is when we take a wrong action and interpret it as good just because something good came out of something that was initially wrong. I believe that all perceived bad things can have a silver lining, but let's not confuse that with the action being right and wrong.

For example, a teenager commits suicide. That is wrong. Because of the teen suicide, it inspires another teen to start an outreach group that ends up preventing ten thousand more suicides. So what that means is the wrongful act of suicide ended up saving ten thousand other teens. As great as this silver lining is, it does not make the original teen suicide right. Make sense? This is important to clarify, because if our society does not know what is right or wrong, well, just watch the evening news tonight.

THE BAD SIX

Let's look closer at right and wrong. I think we could all agree that harming ourselves or another human being mentally or physically is wrong. Regardless of the culture you were raised in and regardless of what behaviors you were taught, harming ourselves or another human being mentally or physically is not right. Everyone has that little voice inside that says, "Hey you, don't hurt yourself or other people!"

Whether we lie, cheat, steal, physically destroy, mentally harm, or physically abuse another, all of these actions are hurting ourselves and/or others. They are wrong. Physical abuse includes sexual abuse. Let's call these the Bad Six: Lie, Cheat, Steal, Destroy, Mentally Harm, and Physically Abuse.

However, yes, there is a however. Even some of the Bad Six are not black and white every time. If we are in a situation where the other human being we are interacting with is clearly in violation of the Bad Six listed above, and it comes down to survival, choose survival!

For example, if a soldier is at war and it comes down to kill or be killed, if he wants to live, he had better pull the trigger. If someone is physically abusing you, it is time to fight. If a crazy person has a gun to your head and says, "I will kill you if you don't tell me that the Denver Broncos are the greatest!", if you are crazy yourself and don't believe this, lie! This is a circumstance where a lie will save your life. There are not always absolutes. When it comes to your survival versus moral code, I believe there are some exceptions here. Choose survival!

MORE ETHICS

Morals can get very hypothetical in debates to the point of imagining situations that would just never happen. When it goes this far, it really gets more philosophical and not practical. So let's have some fun. For example, would you steal a bottle of pills if it was the last bottle of lifesaving medication for your dying child and it was not for sale and there was no other way to save him? Would you steal food for your starving family? If you were one of the last ten people to survive a nuclear war and there was only enough food for eight of you, would you kill the other two for the survival of the group? What would you do? What are *your* rules?

Are ethics *always* about your survival? I don't believe so. This is why the topic is so individual. I believe some situations are more important than our own, even if that means our own death. I have a huge respect for our armed services, for example. They are a gigantic part of allowing us to sleep at night without having to worry about our borders being invaded. One thing I have always admired in Marines, for example, is their "no man left behind" tenant. When it comes to loyalty, they have got it! When it comes to bringing an injured Marine out of a hostile situation, they place more importance on loyalty than their own survival. That is remarkable. How far would you take your loyalty? Would you run in front of a bus to protect your family? Would you jump into an icy river and risk your own life to save another human life? Would a fireman climb into a burning building to save another human being from death? I think we all know the answer to that one. Hats off to all of the service men and women out there who risk their lives every day for others. You are remarkable and admired.

Once again, the reason morality is not black and white is because there are so many different variables and factors that clear black and white rules cannot be set. Often when we talk about character traits like responsibility, pride, and courage, ethical situations can get very blurred. If you are the captain and the ship is sinking, do you stay on and drown so you can show your responsibility and courage? After all of these examples it proves why some ethics are so individual. I think many people would be surprised on just how courageous they can be in actual life or death situations. I believe we are experiencing a time where courage is abound.

Board games have even been created on these hypothetical questions. They can be very challenging to explore, but once again, not very black and white. Life is not black and white. Why don't, as a society, we start with this: *Don't harm yourself or others mentally or physically.* Let's all agree to start with this one and if we get into one of these hypothetical situations, choose survival of yourself *and* survival of the greater good.

So here is the Elevate moral code to determine right and wrong.

1. Does the act hurt ourselves or another human being mentally or physically?

2. Does the act put us in a situation of survival of ourselves or survival of the greater good?

SITUATIONAL ETHICS VERSUS SITUATIONAL CHARACTER

Contrary to popular belief, morality *is* relative based on the situation. There is such a thing as situational ethics and it is right. Situational ethics are what they sound like, ethics which may change during the situation, as stated above. Now character is different. This is where we get confused. Character is not situational or relevant.

If the same person, for example, is a Republican around Republicans and a Democrat around Democrats, that is relative character. That is wrong and slimy. Character is never relative or situational, ethics are. Character is your rock. If it begins to turn into a slippery slope, consider that as feedback that it will not help you get what you want. Even if it does help you get what you want temporarily, you don't want your own soul against you. It won't last. Have you ever met someone who appears hugely successful on the outside, but they can't look you in your eyes, and seem suppressed? That inability is a character issue. Help them. They deserve it. People are good. We all get off track at times.

MORE RIGHT AND WRONG

How about the less obvious rights and wrongs? The highly debated ones: euthanasia, capital punishment, homosexuality, gambling, lust and envy, abortion, pride, premarital sex, animal abuse, recreational and prescription drugs, and alcohol. How about other highly debated moral issues such as: environment, gun control, welfare, and health care? All of these topics are really where we get divided as a society. People in general have very strong emotional opinions to each of these. Below, I share some of my viewpoints, and remember, your view does not have to be my view. Let's agree to avoid the Bad Six and respect each other's opinions on all the other topics. The topics in this section will never be agreed upon by all because they are too individual. The way we feel about each of these is based on what we were each individually taught or based on our own individual experiences. Just knowing this can give you a better understanding on why so many of us differ in our opinion regarding these issues.

For example, if you were raised on a farm and your family produced organic vegetables through sustained farming methods, your opinion is probably going to be pro-environment. If you were raised with a homosexual brother, your opinion is going to probably be pro-gay. If your family was held at gunpoint by a robber in your home, your opinion on gun control is probably going to be pro-gun. Our entire perception of our reality is based on what we were taught and what experiences we have had. We all come from different backgrounds, upbringings, and cultures. Our reality and our opinion of these different topics are shaped by all of our different backgrounds, upbringings, and cultures. This understanding helps to be respectful toward others points of view.

Let's look at each of these individually by asking ourselves questions related to each topic. We are no longer talking about harming another human being or being put in a situation of survival. The purpose of this section is to intelligently approach these issues and gain our own certainty in these areas. Be clear on what you believe. When you have certainty, you have sanity. Indecision is insanity.

Apathy is your enemy.

Apathy, not caring one way or the other, is no longer an option. It's not an option for leaders. Apathy is your enemy.

As a side note, with regards to some of these topics, you may have heard that anything that has the potential to be addictive is a wrong in your life. I have to disagree on this generality. Anything that is addictive we need to take a very close look at, for sure. Just because something has the potential to be addictive, does not make it an automatic wrong. Most of us can enjoy things that can be potentially addictive and not get addicted. Eating too many cream-filled donuts causes obesity. This doesn't mean you can't enjoy a cream-filled donut. I think this all depends on what potential activity we are talking about and the degree of its addictiveness and consequences.

For example, crack cocaine and nicotine are highly addictive, whereas moderate alcohol is typically not. Most of us know ourselves enough to know whether or not we get easily addicted. The key is to make things your servant, not your master, and to recognize the difference. Addiction is an increasing desire for an activity that gives less and less satisfaction. If that is beginning to happen, then stop immediately before it becomes a full-fledged addiction. Know yourself enough to be able to gauge what you are willing to experience. Like I said before, don't experiment with crack cocaine or nicotine, for example. Addictive activities can destroy your life. Your job is to recognize your own tolerance level.

So let's get back to ethical topics that divide us as a society. Let's dive into these controversial topics of individual right and wrong. Begin to get certain on where you stand at this point in your life on each issue. Here we go.

Euthanasia:

The word euthanasia comes from the Greek word, "thanatos," which means death. Directly translated, euthanasia means "good death." If someone was dying of a painful disease and wanted a doctor to end their life, this is defined as euthanasia. Is it a person's choice to end their life through medical intervention? Is euthanasia different from suicide? Is the person contemplating euthanasia in a sane state of mind in order to make that decision? What is your opinion regarding euthanasia?

Capital Punishment:

If someone is unwilling to get rehabilitated back into society and vows to kill again, is capital punishment an option? If someone is willing to get rehabilitated after a crime has been committed, is capital punishment an option? Would you ever allow capital punishment? Why or why not?

Homosexuality:

Is homosexuality right or wrong? Is gay marriage right or wrong? Regardless whether or not we think of homosexuality as being right or wrong, is it okay with you that any class of Americans not be given equal rights such as marriage? How about homosexual couples having children? I once was asked by a gay man, "Why do people care so much about what I choose to do in my bedroom?" I know it is bigger than this; however, that may be a question worth asking.

When I was a teenager I was going to a very, very fundamental church. "Homosexuality is an abomination!" our preacher would shout. I know where many churchgoers are coming from as they battle this topic of "the Bible says ..." As I began to study the Bible more and began relating the scripture to the culture of the time and the reason it was written, it really opened up my spiritual path. Many churches now have gay support groups. These groups explore the Bible and different interpretations of it.

If you are uncertain about the homosexual community and it is Bible-based, I would invite you to contact a church that supports this community and ask them to explore the Bible with you regarding this topic. Where do you stand regarding the homosexual debate?

Gambling:

Can a responsible person gamble recreationally? Can people really limit themselves responsibly? Can gambling be described as expensive entertainment? What is your opinion on gambling?

Lust and Envy:

Lust and envy can take on many forms. Lust is an intense desire or craving. For example, it can mean a lust for knowledge, a lust for sex, or even a lust for power. If we desire to have something intensely, and we are not happy until we get it, it is defined as lust. If we intensely desire something that is not ours, it is defined as envy. Envy means that someone has something that you want yourself to have and not them. Is it okay to have anything in your life that causes such intense desire that it begins to control you? Can a strong lust or envy push out everything and everyone else? Where do you stand on lust or envy?

Abortion:

Is a fetus a human being? Is it a life? If the baby could not survive outside of the mother's womb before six months, is abortion ending the fetus' life? Is it ending its future life? Is it the choice of the mother to abort a growing fetus? How about pregnancy from incest or rape? This does represent an extremely small percentage of abortions, but ask yourself the question. Are you okay with abortion from pregnancies conceived through incest or rape? How about pregnancies that could result in the death of the mother? Once again, this situation represents an extremely small percentage of abortions. How about unborn babies with severe disease? What is your opinion on abortion?

Pride:

Is it wrong to be proud? Can pride be taken too far? Is it important to feel a sense of accomplishment for your hard work? When pride becomes being stuck in our ways and being egotistical, is it okay? When is pride okay for you and when is it not?

Premarital Sex:

Have you ever heard the viewpoint, "Sex is natural outside of marriage. Animals have sex all the time and they are not in committed relationships. Watch monkeys on the discovery channel. They aren't married." Have you also heard the viewpoint, "Yes, but we are not wild animals. We have emotional intelligence, and we do not pick bugs out of each other's skin." If you have a son or daughter, are you okay with them engaging in recreational sex? Is there a difference between premarital sex and promiscuity? Where do you stand in regards to premarital sex?

Animal Abuse:

Is it ever okay to hurt an animal? Do animals have feelings and do they have pain? Are they capable of love? Just because we are a superior species in intelligence and ingenuity, does that mean we can be inhumane to animals? Is there a difference between being inhumane to animals and being humane to animals when killing them for food?

Recreational Drugs and Alcohol:

What about marijuana? Colorado, along with a few other states, legalized medical marijuana a few years ago. An individual needed to get a prescription from a doctor to purchase it. They got a prescription from having a medical diagnosis. And if you live in one of these states, it was amazing how many young adults seemed to be struggling with back pain. Colorado has now legalized recreational marijuana, which has eliminated the need for medical use only.

Is marijuana use wrong? Does it kill brain cells? Does it help some people concentrate? Do you feel it is a good option for pain? Have you seen marijuana completely take friends and family off track by allowing it to rob them of their potential? Have you seen the opposite? If someone is satisfied by getting high all the time, is there any motivation to do anything else? Can an adult use marijuana for recreational purposes in moderation? Is that their choice? Have studies shown it to be more or less dangerous than alcohol or prescription drugs? Are you okay experimenting with something that has the ability to take you off track? Where do you stand regarding marijuana use?

Can you drink alcohol responsibly as an adult? When used recreationally with others, can alcohol be enjoyable, not only for its taste, but for its physiological effects? Does it have health benefits?[2] If you drink and you are not in control of your body, have you had too much? If you regularly drink alone, are you having too much? Can alcohol be dangerous? Where do you stand regarding alcohol use?

Prescription Drugs:

As a doctor, I must share my opinion on this topic. I absolutely, one hundred percent believe that prescription drugs are a last resort. When we cover up our symptoms with drugs or reverse our physiology with drugs, the body gets toxic. This system of health care does not work long term. No matter what you hear on the TV or radio, there is no such thing as a drug without side effects. Properly prescribed medications kill more people a year than illegal drugs hands down.[3] I could go on and on about prescription drug statistics. If you want to see for yourself, look it up online. I believe they should be avoided as much as possible unless your life depends on it or in case of an emergency. I have never met a doctor that would disagree with changing your lifestyle before taking medications, if that was an option. I share my opinion on this because this can save your life. Where do you stand on prescription drugs?

Environment:

What are your views regarding saving the planet? Is it your responsibility to take care of the home we all live on? What do you think? Can you start here: reuse, recycle, and conserve? How do you feel about SUVs? Can a person still love the environment and drive a Hummer? Can a person drive a Prius and continue to have a big carbon footprint?

I have always been surprised by the perception that the Hummer is the poster child for people who don't care about the environment. This is not the truth in most cases. Hummer drivers can still be very conscious of the environment and have a low overall carbon footprint. I happen to own a Hummer, so I know I am a little biased on this one. When it comes to the environment, which areas are important to you? What are your stances regarding the environmental issues?

Gun Control:

What are your views regarding gun control? Whew, this one has really heated up. Do high-powered guns make it easier for sick people to kill numerous innocent people? Our world does make and sell guns that are only made to kill people in war, and some of these are sold to civilians. These guns are not for target practice or for hunting an animal; they are made to kill other people in war. So knowing that, is the problem the sick people or the guns?

Did you know that many of the shooters who kill innocent people in public are on mind-altering, chemical-induced prescription drugs? Some ninety percent of school shootings over more than a decade have been linked to a widely prescribed type of antidepressant.[4] These shootings were committed by disturbed people who were taking mind-altering prescription medications. They were disconnected from reality, folks. Is the problem the guns or the people? Do you know how easy it is to get a prescription for chemically mind-altering antidepressants?

Is it true that guns don't kill people, sick people kill people? Would you ask a woman who has been sexually assaulted to not carry a gun with a conceal carry permit if she wanted to? Do Americans have the right to bear arms? Could we use some regulation over the assault weapons? If you own guns, can you keep your guns locked up in a safe away from your children and teenagers, use them responsibly with care, stay off mind-altering drugs, and carry on? What is your stance regarding gun control?

Welfare:

How do you feel about welfare? Do you believe it is a good form of temporary help or no solution at all? Do you see it as an entitlement or a temporary solution? Does welfare come down to the character of the individual receiving it? If someone receiving welfare feels it is their entitlement as an American and they want to use the system as long as they can, can they do that? If someone receiving welfare feels they are a productive member of society and needs help and are doing everything they possibly can to get productive again, can they do that? Did you know that when welfare was introduced, it had to be paid back? Is welfare highly misused? Do you believe that many people need help at some point in their life? Do you subscribe to the notion that welfare is to help people who are willing to help themselves or cannot help themselves? What is your stance regarding welfare?

Health Care:

What are your views regarding health care? This one is particularly hot right now. New laws have passed that will provide every American with health care. How we as Americans are paying for it is the big divider. I am going to share my opinion on this one. The answer is not more of the modern model of health care. The answer is not more of a health care system that is based on taking drugs for symptoms. The answer to our health care system is not molding it around the multi-billion dollar pharmaceutical industry.

In America, we live in one of the sickest nations in the world. As you can see, we are getting healthier and healthier by taking more and more drugs, wrong! In 2009 alone, the increase of prescription drug use among *children* was nearly four times higher than the overall population, making children the leading growth demographic for the drug industry.[5] Hmmmm. I wonder why we are so sick. We have been programmed since the time we were kids to think that to get healthy, we should cover up our symptoms with medication. It's time to wake up, America. Our modern model of health care is not working!

In 2013, the National Institutes of Health asked the National Academics of Science to compare the health of Americans to people in Canada, Australia, Japan and 13 European countries, including Britain, France, Portugal, Italy, and Germany. It was found that we die earlier from obesity and heart disease than people in the other countries. We spend far more on health care than people in other rich countries, yet have poorer health. We spend more than twice as much money a year per person on health care compared to Britain, France, and Sweden, yet we don't live any longer and we are not healthier. We have more infant mortality, drug abuse, obesity, diabetes, heart disease, lung disease, and disabilities. It has been stated that something fundamentally is going wrong to cause our country to lose ground against other high-income countries.[6] No kidding. Let's change our approach.

When we take care of our health from a proactive approach versus a reactive approach, we will have the answer to our country's health care problem. When we ignore our bodies' symptoms and then take drugs to cover them up, it is early death. Our bodies were designed to live eighty to one hundred and twenty years. It's time to stop creating suicide by our lifestyles.

CONCLUSION

We really dove into some very controversial topics here. As I said earlier, you may or may not agree with my viewpoint on a few of the opinions I shared and that is okay. The main point of this section was to establish a solid moral code regarding the Bad Six. I think we can agree that every one of the Bad Six: Lying, Cheating, Stealing, Mentally Harming, Physically Destroying, and Physically Abusing another, is wrong. The other topics are harder. What is important is that you are certain on what you believe to be the truth in those areas and at the same time, know you are open to learning about different rational viewpoints, and then respect the opinions of others if they differ from yours. Wouldn't life be a little boring if we all had the same opinion anyway? Some things are black and white, some are very gray.

> **Bottom line:** When it comes to moral code, don't harm yourself or others mentally or physically. When it comes to survival, choose survival. Avoid the Bad Six and find your truth for the other topics. Some morals are relative to the situation and to the individual. Character is not.

4Chapter Four:
Forgiveness of Self and Others

"Resentment is like drinking poison and
waiting for the other person to die."
-Carrie Fisher

I think the above quote says it all. Unforgiveness of our self or others is like growing a spreading cancer in our bodies that we have the choice to cure, and yet some of us refuse to do it. What is unforgiveness? The definition of unforgiveness is the act of choosing not to give up resentment you harbor toward another or yourself. We all know that resentment truly is like us drinking poison and expecting the other person to get hurt. It is just not a productive emotion to get what you want. Leaders forgive. Winners forgive. They move forward. Winners learn from the action. Carrying resentment around with you is like growing your fortune with tons of bad debt. It is very difficult and does not serve us for the better.

As an entrepreneur, I have done several deals. Some of them turned out well, others not so well, and one scandalous. In my mid-twenties I wired ninety thousand dollars to an investor I had never met, to invest in a private placement memorandum for an up-and-coming national coffee shop. I thought I had done my due diligence, but apparently not enough. I had been burned, along with many others, by a professional scam artist. He checked out on everything I knew to check. I had friends that had even done deals with him. After the lawsuit, it was obvious that, one, attorneys are expensive and, two, I was not going to see a dime of my money. I do love my attorney, by the way! Have you heard that good judgment comes from experience? Well, bad judgment comes from lack of experience. I certainly suffered from lack of experience on this one.

I was angry; ninety thousand dollars is a large amount of money. The scam artist never went to jail, and many years later I received a call from an investigator that was reviewing him and his background to allow him to take over a family trust. After my conversation with the investigator, I hope they had enough information to obviously not put him in that position of authority.

This happened over ten years ago. I did forgive him. I blamed myself and took responsibility for making the poor decision. I thought I was over it; however, I was recently clearing out my filing cabinet, and I came across all of the legal papers and original documents regarding that deal. I admit that I had a small burst of revenge shoot through my veins, "It's been ten years. No one would ever expect me to be the cause of his untimely beating while he comes home from the grocery store. Muhuhahahaha!" Needless to say, I had the opportunity to put my forgiveness to the test once again. I took a deep breathe, forgave him and myself again, and shredded all evidence of his existence.

What has happened to you? What's your forgiveness story?

FORGIVENESS OF SELF

What have you done that still has you prisoner in your mind? Are you carrying around the emotion of guilt based on something you did in the past? Let's walk through this together. Unforgiveness of yourself is a trap that will keep you down and will absolutely block you from experiencing the most possible joy out of every day. Guilt will keep you suppressed and certainly won't keep you in a state of mind to get what you want.

Ask yourself what still has a negative emotional charge in your mind? What are you feeling guilty about? What did you do? It's time to set this aside and let yourself know that guilt is better thought of as intelligent regret. You may have done something you are feeling regretful about, and now you can intelligently look at that and fix it! Have you heard that you should never feel guilty? Let's look at this closer. If you go against your moral code, it is healthy to feel that emotion of, "Oops, I shouldn't have done that." This is healthy. What we choose to do with that emotion is what makes the emotion of guilt destructive or productive. When we know we have done something wrong toward ourselves or others, it is good to recognize that. How we interpret and respond to it is the key.

So number one, you must forgive yourself of past actions. Here are some steps that will help.

1. Determine, specifically, what you did that you feel bad about. Recognize that the past action is causing you negative feelings.

2. Accept that up until now, you have been living in a constant state of unforgiveness toward yourself and it is no longer serving you.

3. Ask yourself what you were thinking, what your mindset was, or where you were coming from, when you performed the action for which you are seeking forgiveness.

4. Admit to yourself that as a human being you are a work in progress. You are a good person. You are God's creation and you are meant to shine. Admit that you are not perfect, will never be perfect, and you will probably perform actions again in the future that you will not be proud of. It is part of life. It is how we grow as people. You are getting better and better.

5. If the action was not performed against yourself, and was performed against someone else, contact the person you need to contact and tell them you are sorry and figure out how to make it right if you can. (I know this is a hard one, but you are worth it!)

6. Lastly, let it go. Release it. No matter how it goes with the other person, forgive yourself and move forward. Once it is off your chest, regardless of how the other person feels, know that you have admitted your mistake, attempted to make it right, and that is all you can do.

These steps will set you free. I know they are not easy. Forgiveness of yourself is one of the hardest things a person can ever do. Some people reading this may not even make it past this chapter. I urge you, if you are not forgiving yourself of something, please move forward and make it right. Forgive yourself. You are worth it. You are worth it. You are worth it.

If you still want to hold on to the negative emotion of not forgiving yourself, then I bet you have a hard time forgiving others as well. We are about making the world better here. This is a movement. Let it go. Let it go for your sake and for others around you. Carrying around negative guilt is bitterness, agitation, short temper, and early death. If you need help, seek it out. There is a better way to get what you want from life, and not forgiving yourself is not acceptable. Unwillingness to forgive yourself becomes an issue that is no longer about you, but about others you interact with. It is not only about you now; it is also about others. Remember, God wants you to shine His light. Unforgiveness is darkness encompassing everything you do. Forgive yourself and move on.

FORGIVENESS OF OTHERS

For some of you, forgiving yourself was a breeze, and for others, not so much. If it was hard, keep after it. Now, on to forgiveness of others. Hold on there, cowboy! This one might be a little bit harder. It is important to forgive yourself first so you can create that understanding that you *can* forgive others. Hey, if we are all works in progress, and you can forgive yourself, then maybe, just maybe, you can go through a similar process and forgive others. Have you ever been granted forgiveness from someone else? Can we pay it forward and do the same?

My business attorney told me one time, "Everybody has self-interests, and other people's self-interests may not be the same as your self-interests." I thought that was great. Strive to be proactive the next time someone trespasses against you. Expecting the best in people doesn't mean you shouldn't also accept the worst-case scenario. To recognize that others' self-interests may not be the same as your self-interests helps take the emotion out of a situation that you feel you were crossed with. Not everyone has one hundred percent integrity. Many times what is perceived as an attack against you is that person's process of becoming a better person. The person that crossed you may still be learning the fundamentals of the Big Six: Honesty, Respect, Loyalty, Faith, Courage, and Love. It is totally out of your control. If you act with one hundred percent integrity, then most of the time, others will also when dealing with you.

So who did what to you? What are you still upset about? How is carrying that around going for you? I understand that forgiving Johnny for stealing your lunch money may be much, much easier than forgiving your spouse for adultery. I understand that forgiving that stranger that door dinged your car may be much, much easier than forgiving the man that molested your child. There are certainly various degrees of how easy or difficult the process of forgiveness is. My hope is that regardless of the circumstance you need to forgive, it is becoming more clear that resentment will not get you to your greatness. Resentment is continuing to swallow that poisonous pill, expecting the other person to die. Resentment and unforgiveness steals your light, not theirs. Are you going to let them hurt you twice? Once with the action they performed against you and now for the rest of your life? You know what to do.

If you need to forgive someone else, let's go through some steps together.

1. Determine what action was performed against you that has a negative charge.

2. Accept that up until now, you have been living in a state of unforgiveness toward others and it is no longer serving you.

3. Ask yourself what they were thinking or where they possibly could have been coming from, when they delivered the action you are feeling resentful about.

4. Admit to yourself that, as human beings, we are all works in progress. Admit that no one is perfect; no one will ever be perfect. Hurt people hurt others.

5. If you have the ability, contact the person you need to contact and ask them where they were coming from or what were they thinking at the time the action took place. Seek to understand them. If you do not have this opportunity, write them a letter that you will never send them because they are either dead or not contactable.

6. Ask yourself how this action that you are forgiving served you in life. How has it made you better? *What?* Yes. This can be challenging, but keep digging. The action happened. Pull out the positive. How has it made you better? How did it serve you?

7. Ask yourself if you have ever done something similar to someone else at some point in your life. If you have, recognize it. If you have not, move forward.

8. Lastly, let it go. Release it. No matter how it goes with the other person, forgive them and move forward. Once it is off your chest, regardless of where the other person was coming from, you have admitted your resentment and have to let it go.

THE ADVERSITY IN FORGIVENESS

In step six above, I asked, "How has the negative action performed against you served you?" How did the action make you a better person? Once you get clear on how the action actually made you a better person, this can sometimes totally abolish any feelings of resentment or unforgiveness. When someone performs an act against us, it can create strength if we allow it to. Whatever doesn't kill us makes us

> When someone performs an act against us, it can create strength if we allow it to.

43

stronger, right? Remember, in the moral code chapter, if something wrong happened to us, it is how we perceive it that makes it good or bad. For example, if Joe, we'll call him Joe, if Joe hadn't been beat up in high school, he never would have developed the drive to become a mixed martial artist world champion. Instead of wanting to forgive his bully, he would want to thank him! Can anything that you still need to forgive be completed with a silver lining?

Personally, I was raised by my single mom. We struggled financially tremendously, and I ended up attending thirteen different elementary schools. I didn't realize how abnormal this was until I was giving a motivational speech at a transitional homeless shelter. I was doing my best encouraging them, giving them hope, and sharing my story. They ended up coming up to me and telling me how sorry they were for me! Huh? I didn't get it. I became angry about it and confronted my mom regarding the program of instability that was downloaded to me as a child. Through the process of forgiveness, I realized that, one, I was very loved and she did the very best she could, and, two, having the experience of being the new kid at thirteen elementary schools gave me the skills of being able to connect and meet friends quickly, as well as feeling comfortable speaking to groups. Every perceived bad action that happened to us can have a silver lining if we choose it to. Happiness in life is not about what happens to us, it is about how we interpret what happens to us.

TURN THE OTHER CHEEK

Many of us have heard the biblical scripture that says to "turn the other cheek." This one has really challenged me. You might say, "Turn the other cheek? What? If someone hit me in the cheek, I'm knocking them out!" I believe what Jesus meant was, if someone hurts you, show them unconditional love, defend yourself, and show them that the anger cycle stops with you. This doesn't mean to not hit them back to stop the attack, by the way. To me it means to get the situation under control and show them that the violence stops with you.

His lesson was a lesson that hurting people hurt people, and we *can* be the light. Show them the way through our example. This level is super tenth degree black belt spirituality, by the way. Don't test someone if you don't want to get smacked!

FORGIVE OR FORGET

We have all heard forgive and forget, and many times this is very valid. We need to expand on this one a little. Depending on the severity of the action we were resentful about, sometimes we need to forgive and not be so fast to forget. For example, if you left your purse out next to a coworker and that coworker stole your purse, then even though everything was forgiven and made right, don't leave your purse out around them again. I know there are varying degrees of this; however, there is a difference between unconditional love and being naive. There is a difference between being blindly positive and being cautiously optimistic. If a convicted child molester has sought forgiveness and paid his dues, it doesn't mean I am going to let my children spend the night at his house. This is called being smart.

Don't confuse this with "never trust others." We should always expect the best in others unless they give us a reason not to. If you have been burned before from someone, let it go, move forward with a clean slate.

Expect the best in others and at the same time it is okay to be prepared for the worst. It is okay to trust and verify. The worst thing we can do is generalize all people because we were treated a certain way by one person. For example, "I don't trust men because I was physically abused by my first boyfriend." or "I don't trust women because I was cheated on in college." This will not serve you. Forgive, forgive, forgive, and YES, forget in those situations. When I say forgive and be slow to forget, I am referring to a particular person, not a generalization of people. Yes, we should forgive our enemies but do not forget their names. Screw me once, shame on you. Screw me twice, shame on me.

> **Bottom line:** Forgive yourself and others. Forgiveness is about getting over it for your sake. Let it go and unleash your best. Be emotionally free and break the shackles of unforgiveness and resentment. You are worth it.

Elevate

Chapter Five:
Self-Acceptance and Seeking Approval

"I stopped caring so much about what other people thought about me until I realized how little they did."

-Rob Rohe

I love myself! I love myself! I love myself! YOUR TURN. Stop reading, go in front of a mirror, look into your eyes and say, "I love myself, I love myself, I love myself." Seriously, stop reading and do this exercise. Don't read the next paragraph because it will rob you of this wonderful life lesson. Ready, set, go. Find a mirror, and say to yourself, "I love myself! I love myself! I love myself!" Do it now.

Okay, survey says: the results of this exercise are based on how you *felt* when you said it. So how did it feel? Did it make you feel good, sad, uncertain, or silly? Answer that question now. Did it make you feel good, sad, uncertain, or silly?

You just gave yourself the self-acceptance check-up. The way you felt immediately following that exercise is your starting point. If you felt good, great, let's make you feel even better. If you felt bad, great, now we know we have some work to do. If you felt uncertain or silly, excellent, we have a great deal of room to grow here.

If you have some work to do in this category, and believe me, all of us do, then let's get started. Let's focus on self-acceptance. One of the main clutches of unhappiness is to not accept ourselves exactly as we are. Most advertisements help us feel this way. For many of us, we are too fat, too skinny, our hair is too curly, too straight, either too much or not enough of this, that and everything else. When we tell ourselves that we are not good enough, we create the *feeling* of not being good enough. And that feeling does not work!

It's time to stop sabotaging our happiness by being in agreement with the loser voice in our heads. We all have two voices, and they go by different names: the angel and the devil, the winner and the weenie, the encourager and the defeater, the "go for it" and the "don't even think about it." Which one do you choose most of the time?

The key is to accept yourself exactly as you are. Even if you don't enjoy a particular trait, accept it! This is who you are right here, right now. This is step one. Love all of yourself, right or wrong, good or bad, love it. This is you, baby. You were made to be a work in progress. That's one of the purposes in life! If we were perfect, what would be the point? We *find* ourselves through our growth. We reach new heights by pushing through the resistance. This is what being your best is all about.

Accept yourself right now for who you are, what you have done, how you look, and how you treat others. Through and through, love yourself right now for everything you are and everything you stand for. Can you do that? If yes, keep reading. If no, reread the Forgiveness of Self and Others chapter. Seriously. This book is meant to be a step-by-step action plan to achieve whatever you want in life. I believe in you!

AUTHENTICITY

My favorite self-acceptance trait has to be authenticity. I love when someone has total and complete acceptance of themselves. It shows not only in their confidence levels, but also in their ability to relate and be compassionate toward others. Aren't the people closest to you the ones that you can be the most vulnerable with?

Authenticity breaks down barriers. Most everyone appreciates it because so many of us want to be able to have more of it. If you want an instant connection with others, be authentic. If you share some of your challenges, they will see that you are sincere and they will want to share some of their challenges with you. Together you can help each other *Elevate*! And by the way, if you ever do open up to someone and show your vulnerability and authenticity and then they do not reciprocate, or pretend that they have not been challenged by anything similar, then give them a copy of this book. They need it!

For example, folks, I physically have a big head. I know it and I have known it for a long time. I love my head. I like to think that the reason my head is so big is because I have a big brain. I also have a turkey neck. You know, the kind of neck that slopes down directly from your chin. I have a turkey neck and am very proud of it. It comes from my Hungarian grandfather. I like to think that having a gobble, gobble turkey neck is my reminder that if I want to soar with the eagles, I can't hang out with the turkeys! I also have big cheeks! My big cheeks take up most of my face!

These traits really have been blessings. My big head, big cheeks and turkey neck have served as great gifts in my life. For example, when I fall off track and not follow my nutrition and exercise plan, my face and chin get fat! Oh, I'm totally serious. I can't even hide an extra five pounds because when I get five pounds overweight, two pounds go in each cheek and one pound goes right to my neck! I already have a big head; now add five pounds of fat to my face! Whoa, I'm talking, wowza!

Another personal self-acceptance example is my recurring stutter. I developed a stutter at a young age after my parents divorced. I went through many sessions of school-sponsored speech therapy as a child and got it under control. Two of the syllables I struggled with were pronouncing my K's and J's. My first name is Keppen, my wife's name is Jennifer, and my two boys are named Jay and Karson! Talk about K's and J's. Talk about conquering fear. Seriously, it was pretty bad as a child. I wanted to change my name to Mike just so I could pronounce my damn name.

I am happy to say that while I do not stutter anymore, it does creep up once in a while as a gift. If I am very uncertain about a direction in my life or a certain situation, I start to stammer with my words. It is my friendly reminder to get certain and get certain now! I could go on with a few more things that I have accepted about myself, but you get the picture.

What do you need to accept about yourself? Everyone has something they need to accept about themselves. Put a little humor behind it and you won't turn back. If you're not having fun, you're not doing it right. Self-deprecating humor is very healthy when it comes from a place of power and self-acceptance. Do you want to get what you want? Accept yourself now!

NEED TO RECOGNIZE

Sometimes we need help in even realizing *what it is* that we need to accept in ourselves. One good tool is to recognize if there is anything in anyone else that you can't stand. I mean, you really, really don't like. "When I get around this person, I hate it when they act like that!" or "I don't know what it is, but I really despise that person." If you can relate to this, you have just discovered a wonderful gift. Here it is: Whatever trait we are not yet willing to accept in our own lives is the same trait we cannot stand to be around in others. That is big.

Begin to ask yourself what you can't stand in others *and* ask yourself where it is *also* in your life.

For example, "I can't stand being around Jimmy. He is so pompous and thinks he knows everything." Where does this show up in your life?

49

Where do you portray self-righteousness and overcompensate with too much pride? "Well, hold on a second," you might say. "What if I can't stand physical abusers? Are you saying I am a physical abuser? I don't abuse people!" Well, isn't physical abuse an ultimate form of disrespect? Are you *disrespecting* anyone in your life that you need to get a gut check on?

Or how about, "I can't stand racists! I'm not a racist!" That may be true; however, what is racism? It is ignorance. It is a lack of self-acceptance. It may be a sign of unforgiveness because they were hurt by someone in that race. It is disrespect. It is hate. Which trait do you need to work on?

Just because you recognize the trait in someone doesn't mean you haven't accepted yourself in this area. What you are looking for is a strong emotional charge that leaves you very angry or stressed when you interact with them based on the trait they portrayed. *This* is your sign that you have the opportunity for growth.

You know you have figured it out once you are put in that situation again. You will recognize it as something you don't like; however, your emotional charge to it is gone. You will know you have mastered this tool when you see *everyone* as works in progress, including yourself, especially yourself.

This also works in a positive, reaffirming way. Whatever you admire in others is what you want more of in your life. The next time you get inspired by someone or by a movie actor, for example, what character traits did that person or movie actor portray? How do those same character traits measure up in your life? This is an awesome tool. So remember this wonderful gift: Whatever you admire in others is what you seek more of for yourself.

We are all on the path of self-growth whether you recognize it or not.

When you can't stand something in someone else, it is your opportunity to grow. When you are inspired, it is your opportunity to grow. We all go through the same lessons eventually. How fast you want to get what you want is up to you. How fast you want to grow through these pillars of self-growth is up to you. The reason we are able to see someone who is not responsible, for example, is because we had that trait in ourselves and we had to learn the pillar of self-responsibility.

We are all on the path of self-growth whether you recognize it or not. The fast track is up to you. The reason recovered drug addicts can pick out other drug addicts so easily is because they have gone through it themselves. As we go through life, we can see others' shortcomings as aggravations and become self-righteous, or we can see others' shortcomings as opportunities to relate and help them if they want it.

JUDGMENT

This is the cure to judgment. Next time you judge someone, ask yourself if you have ever done the same thing or something similar at some point in your life? This question puts you in a leadership position to relate to them, not judge them. The next time you hear gossip or witness non-confrontation, or see someone blame someone else, take it as an opportunity to relate and help them win. There are so many reasons people will judge you; it is impossible to have control over that. People judge others because of their own low self-esteem and of their own lack of self-acceptance. It is a non-serving program that some of us use to make ourselves feel temporarily better. "They must be terrible, so I feel better about myself now." This doesn't work long term.

SEEKING APPROVAL

A while back, I was in a group environment where I got to know the others over the course of a weekend. A nice woman came up to me at the end of the weekend and said, "You know, at first I didn't like you, but now I like you." Frankly, it kind of threw me off. I did a gut check. What did I do? What would I do to make you not like me? I examined myself. I stepped back and examined my moral code. "Did I act in a way that was not congruent with my Big Six character traits?" I was searching for a reason to apologize to her if I needed to. In this situation, I couldn't find one. If I had crossed her wrongly in some way, I would have apologized. I realized that her statement had nothing to do with me.

When you realize that seeking approval from others is an impossible challenge, you won't participate in it anymore. You will never get everyone to like everything you do, let alone get one person to like everything you do. The only one you need to seek approval from is yourself. When you are negatively judged, why would you care what others thought of you, especially when the opinion of the person who gave the judgment probably has a poor opinion of themselves?

What if a bank teller just got in trouble with her boss and was in a bad mood as a result. You come in smiling and she ends up treating you poorly. It had nothing to do with you. What if that same bank teller just won five thousand dollars from a scratch ticket and was in a good mood as a result. You come in smiling and she ends up treating you really well. Her mood before you got there had nothing to do with you. Don't get stuck in seeking approval from others based on their moods and how they treat you. It usually has nothing to do with you.

"Why do I care so much about what someone else thinks about me? Why is it so challenging for me to be totally independent of the good or bad opinion of others?" If you are asking these questions, you are human. It simply means you still are getting to know who you are and what you stand for. All of us ask these questions at some point in our lives. They are healthy questions to ask. Until we have total acceptance of ourselves, we will continue to seek acceptance of others.

CONSTRUCTIVE CRITICISM

For clarity, I don't believe we should be *totally* independent of the good or bad opinion of others when we respect who the opinion is coming from. I think feedback from others we respect is important and fundamental. This is called constructive criticism. This is a powerful tool. This is where it is good to be in line with those we respect. To not care about seeking approval from those we respect is like a four-year-old child saying to his loving mother, "I don't care if you don't like my messy hair or spaghetti all over my face. I'm not seeking approval from you." This doesn't work. This is a situation where someone we respect is trying to help us.

I had an employee many years back who was on our marketing and promotion team. She was a strong driver and a classic promoter. She was very dominant and very informal. These types of personalities are really fun to be around but can be very hard to reign in, in business especially. I saw many opportunities in her that she had not yet recognized in herself. I recognized them because I have had them myself. I had to learn those pillars of self-growth, too. Some of the qualities I recognized in her were the need to be right, stubbornness, and being a know-it-all. I liked her and thought it might be an opportunity to help her grow as a leader. As my employee, those character traits were beginning to cause a good deal of grief on my team, so I approached our conversation as a win/win opportunity.

I thought I related to her well and discussed how those traits were not going to help our team or herself long term. They were strong traits that were misguided and could be guided correctly to really help her and our organization. She ended up taking our conversation as me projecting my negative traits on her. This was just not the case. I had no emotional charge to her negative traits. I was truly trying to help her. Instead of seeing our conversation as one that would help her and our organization, she saw it as her need to be right. She is no longer with our company, but I know I at least planted a seed. Hey, we all grow. Your ability to be coachable from others you respect is proportionate to your ability to grow as a person and get what you want.

WHO CARES WHAT OTHERS THINK?

Here are a couple of examples where not caring what others think may be taking it too far. This first example involves connection versus isolation. There is a difference between not caring what others think and not wanting to be part of the herd. If you want to be totally independent of others and want to sing out loud in public places and wear underwear on top of your head, that is great; however, you are trading human connection for it. People who are *completely* independent of the opinion of others are truly unique, this is true, but they also tend to get isolated. When we make ourselves intentionally different from everyone else, not caring at all about social norm, we are telling others that, "I do not want to be like you, and I am not going to connect with you." This is a personal choice. I think it is good to follow social norms and *still* be able to express your uniqueness. Human connection is vital to happiness.

The second example involves relationships. If you are having tension with someone in your life and there has been communication left unsaid, then this is not the time to take the attitude of not caring what they think. This is the time to make sure you have fully understood where they were coming from and to make sure that they have fully understood where you were coming from. Once you have communicated with them and you are confident that they understood what your intent was, then it is time to let it go. If they still hold a grudge, there is nothing else you can do, and it is not about you anymore at that point. Depending on the closeness of the relationship, it then may be time to not care what they think and move on.

BETTER YOURSELF

So now that we have accepted ourselves for who we are, right here, right now, what do you want to change or make better? Yes, this is the kicker. Just because you have accepted yourself doesn't mean you should be in agreement with the things in your life that you are not happy about. Here's what I mean, if you are fat, love yourself just the way you are *and* love yourself enough to take action to become lean. I don't mean to offend you. I've been fat in my life before and it's not healthy.

If your hair is important to you and is damaged, love yourself just the way you are *and* find out what you need to do to restore it. It's important to take care of our hygiene, folks. What is it for you? What *can* you change for the better? Accept yourself as you are and love yourself enough to make the necessary changes you *can make* to feel better.

If there is a trait in your life that you *cannot* change because it is *literally* impossible, then trust in the fact that everything happens for a reason and it is there to serve you and others in some way. God makes no mistakes. You were wonderfully created and were created for a purpose. I know of a three-foot tall man in a wheel chair that has more self-acceptance in his soul than anyone I know. His name is Sean Stephenson. Check out his Dance Party video clip online.

Later, we will go into much more detail about bettering these areas. I will give you the tools you need to successfully tackle the areas of your life that you want to improve. For now, take the mental step in totally, absolutely, one hundred percent accepting yourself. Amen!

> **Bottom line:** If you can't accept yourself, no one else will. Stop seeking approval from others and seek approval from yourself. Once you accept you as you, recognize things in your life that are interfering with full acceptance of yourself and have the courage to make them better. You will be well on your way to saying I LOVE MYSELF and feeling damn good about it.

Chapter Six:
Believe in Yourself

"Our deepest fear is not that we are inadequate. Our deepest fear is that we are powerful beyond measure. It is our light, not our darkness that most frightens us. We ask ourselves, who am I to be brilliant, gorgeous, talented, and fabulous? Actually, who are you not to be? You are a child of God. Your playing small does not serve the world. There is nothing enlightened about shrinking so that other people won't feel insecure around you. We are all meant to shine, as children do. We were born to make manifest the glory of God that is within us. It's not just in some of us; it's in everyone. And as we let our own light shine, we unconsciously give other people permission to do the same. As we are liberated from our own fear, our presence automatically liberates others."

-Nelson Mandela

The four most important words you can tell another human being for encouragement is, "I believe in you!" It feels great to hear, doesn't it? It is empowering to know that someone believes in you! Why do you think that is?

Belief in yourself is a fundamental key skill to live the life you want. We must know down to our bones that we *can* do it, that we have what it takes, and that we have faith we are going to come through in any situation if we ever want to get what we want.

One of Zig Ziglar's famous quotes is, "You can be anything you want to be, have anything you want to have, and do anything you want to do." These affirmative words are life changing. Folks, when you believe in yourself, you have fuel to conquer the many challenges that will come your way. You will develop the power to drive your ambition to achieve anything you want. Belief in yourself is magic to your life.

We all have the light! *This little light of mine, I'm gonna let it shine!* People who shine are the most successful people in the world. People who have a solid belief in themselves accept themselves; they love themselves, and they trust themselves. They have the fuel to achieve greatness because they believe they can! They believe they were made for a bigger purpose than just themselves. They know that living small doesn't benefit anyone. Life is too short to be little! They demand more from themselves than anyone possibly expects! They know that happiness comes from striving to be their ideal selves every day. Belief in ourselves allows us to break the shackles of inhibition! So many of us have lost our belief in ourselves. Guess what? We can get it back!

If you have it already, grow it! If you don't already have it, how do you get this belief in yourself back? Well, it begins when we are kids. It starts with our parents, our best friends, our siblings closest to us. We develop this belief first from encouragement of those we love: "You can do it; I believe in you, Johnny; Way to go; I knew you had it in you; you have everything it takes, Sally!" These words of encouragement set the framework for a life of belief in ourselves.

I must give a shout out to my mom on this one! As I mentioned earlier, we had it pretty rough while I was growing up. It was extremely unstable, to say the least. We ran from one bad situation to another, trying to make a better life. Don't get me wrong, I was a happy kid. I didn't know any different, really. The one thing that was constantly downloaded into me big time though was that I could do anything I set my mind to, regardless of the circumstance. I was told that I was special and had a gift. I was told I could create a different, more stable life for my future family. I took all those pearls of encouragement throughout my childhood and applied them to my life and my wonderful family now. I am grateful for my childhood. It laid the foundation for my drive and grounded me to what truly makes a person happy. Thanks, Mom!

Now if we didn't have the opportunity with loved ones around us growing up, to have positive, encouraging, belief-creating statements downloaded into our heads and hearts, then we start now with ourselves. Some of the most encouraging people I know had some pretty rotten childhoods. They see their childhood experiences as a gift and as a future strength. They see them as an opportunity to realize how important having someone believe in them is. And since they never had it, they are the biggest encouragers I know. So if you didn't get the belief in yourself from a loved one, start now by telling yourself, "Yes, I can do it; Yes, I do believe in myself!" You will get it back!

SELF-ESTEEM

If you really aren't sure how strong your belief in yourself is, then let's test it. Low self-esteem is generally a good indicator of many of our character traits, including a strong belief in ourselves. Ask yourself the following yes or no questions:

1. Am I too sensitive to criticism?

2. Am I extremely hard on myself?

3. Do I not own up to my responsibility?

4. Do I blame others?

5. Do I feel like I am a victim to other people and situations?

6. Do I excessively boast of my accomplishments, or conversely, make excuses for them?

7. Do I feel inferior or superior to others?

8. Do I completely avoid taking risks?

9. Is it hard for me to say no when I need to?

10. Do I often say what people want to hear versus how I really feel?

If you answered yes to any of these questions, guess what? You're human! If you answered yes to *many* of these questions, it's time to fix that low self-esteem. It's time to create a solid belief in yourself. We *all* have varying degrees of low self-esteem at times. Consistent low self-esteem is a symptom from not believing in ourselves. Not believing in ourselves is usually based on consistently making poor choices and not taking responsibility for them. We can recognize it in ourselves because it comes out many times when we are around people that are doing a better job of taking consistent action in their lives than we are. For example, when you see someone who is incredibly fit, do you get crushed inside or do you say to yourself, "That's going to be me soon! I can do it." When you see someone with more wealth than you, do you say to yourself, "Look at that filthy-rich snob!" or do you say, "They must have really worked hard and created value for many people, like I am doing, to achieve such a great accomplishment!" How do you talk to yourself?

Another good measure of how much you believe in yourself is by how well you are treated by others. To believe in yourself is to have value in yourself. Others will treat you the way you treat yourself. If you value yourself, others will value you. Until you value yourself, no one else will. If you don't believe in yourself, no one else will.

In order to develop a solid belief in yourself, you must first decide which side of the fence you would rather be on? Do you want to be a person with low self-esteem or high self-esteem? Do you want to be a person with high belief in yourself or low belief in yourself? I am spending time on self-esteem because without recognizing if it is low or not, we won't have the desire to increase it. Without high self-esteem, there is no true belief in ourselves. Which column do you choose?

LOW SELF-ESTEEM VERSUS HIGH SELF-ESTEEM

Low Self-Esteem	High Self-Esteem
Sees childhood adversity as a lifelong sad story as to why they are the way they are	Sees childhood adversity as a strength and gift
Quick to anger	Doesn't anger easily and seeks first to understand
Self-righteous and stubborn	Open minded and respectful to others' points of view
Overbearing and overcompensating pride	Recognizes pride as a humble harnessed power
Critical of self and others	Non-judgmental and recognizes own fallacies and short comings as improvements that are being worked on
Entitled	Recognizes need to contribute and produce
Constant stress	Prepares for upcoming events to avoid stress in most cases
Demanding attitude	Serving attitude
Chaotic relationships	Solid communicative relationships

HOW DO I BELIEVE IN MYSELF?

The fundamentals of believing in yourself come down to faith and integrity. We will get more into faith in the next chapter; however, start with this: God created you for greatness. He created you for a purpose. You were born to thrive. You were born because He made you to fulfill your destiny and achieve your dreams. You have people to serve with your talents. God believes in you and He is the creator of the entire universe! I would say that is a pretty good source to believe in you! If He believes in you, then how about *you* believe in *you*. Make sense?

We explored integrity in the character chapter. When it comes to integrity, if you are consistently not being congruent with what you say, think, or do, it's not going to help you. When these are out of line, it is impossible to build the foundation of belief in yourself. You must be able to love yourself, accept yourself, and trust yourself to get what you want. Make sure what you think and say are in agreement! What is glaring you in the face right now? What do you think of right away when you ask yourself, "Is what I am thinking, saying, and doing in alignment?" If it is not, begin to work on that first. Be that person! Be the person who does what they say and who says what they think, and watch your belief in yourself soar!

Our minds are our greatest encourager.

Once we get this foundation set of faith and integrity, it's up to us to continue the belief in ourselves with our own positive self-talk. Our minds are our greatest encourager. Examples of positive self-talk are, "I can do this; nothing is going to stop me; I believe in myself; I am strong and courageous." Try saying these now. Feels good, doesn't it?

Our minds talk to us all of the time, remember? We all have that little voice in our head. If you don't think you have a voice in your head, it's the voice that just said, "What voice? I don't hear a voice." Yes, folks, if you have a pulse, you have a voice in your head. So if you are going to talk to yourself, you might as well make it positive! Avoid negative talk completely! At times we say negative things to ourselves that we would never say to somebody else. That is the opposite of believing in ourselves.

If not having a belief in yourself is your source of low self-esteem then let's revisit the ten self-esteem questions. Assuming you said yes to some of them, how can we change your answer?

1. Am I too sensitive to criticism?

   I recognize criticism as either constructive or destructive, based on who is giving me the criticism. If I respect the person's results in their lives, I take their criticism as a willing and coachable athlete would take a coach's wisdom. If I recognize the criticism as judgment from someone I do not respect, then I dismiss it and realize they are really talking about themselves.

2. Am I extremely hard on myself?

   I know that I am a work in progress. If I fail, I pick myself back up and learn from what happened. This makes me more prepared for success the next time. I recognize that being too hard on myself does not serve me and gets in my way of achieving what I want.

3. Do I not own up to my responsibility?

   I am ultimately responsible for everything in my life. When I recognize that I have the ability to respond to everything that comes my way, I live in a state of control over everything I can possibly have control over.

4. Do I blame others?

   I recognize that when I blame, I lose. When I don't own up to what happened it keeps me stuck in the same cycle. I know that to win means to not blame.

5. Do I feel like I am a victim to other people and situations?

   I know that I choose my path. I know that I can control my life, and for the things that I cannot control, I learn from. I control how people treat me by how I show up to the party.

6. Do I excessively boast of my accomplishments, or conversely, make excuses for them?

   I know that a healthy sense of pride is crucial for forward motion. I also know that no one likes to be around a boaster or bragger, and my relationships are important to me. I know that a bad day for my ego is a good day for my soul.

7. Do I feel inferior or superior to others?

   I know that we are all works in progress and if I forget that, life has a way of balancing me out. I know that every person and situation is my teacher. I know that when compared to others, I am better or worse at some things, just like they are.

8. Do I completely avoid taking risks?

   I know that success involves calculated risk. I know that I can't be brave if I am not scared. I know that to be great I must push beyond my comfort zone. I know that all of the fruit is out on the limb.

9. Is it hard'for me to say no when I need to?

   I know that life is much more fun when I say yes versus no; however, I also know that my yes or my no is based on how much control I have over the key areas of my life. If I am getting out of balance, I know when to say no in that area.

10. Do I often say what people want to hear versus how I really feel?

    I know that my feelings count and I am true to expressing them. I know that my opinion counts and I can make a difference by what I have to say.

NO REGRETS

Live the life you have always wanted to live. If not now, when? If not you, then who? Come on! You were destined for greatness. Think like a person that has a high belief in themselves. The road to someday leads to nowhere. The time is now.

I saw a current picture of an old poster cover girl model the other day and she had aged considerably, as we all do. One of her gifts to the world was her outer beauty. Her time had passed with this gift. Have you ever met a retired sixty-year-old NFL player? Their gift had obviously passed, too, hadn't it? Folks, don't put all of your self-esteem in your current talent. You are not only destined for greatness, you are destined for all-time greatness. It may change like beauty or athletic ability does, but you are not your talent. You are much more than that. Be your best and elevate your gifts. Live all out now, because when they fade, they fade. At that point what makes a winner a true winner is to recognize that although their gift to the world did not last forever, their shining light will. It may be reinvention time for the next gift to the world. The time is always now!

I hope that by the time we are in our rocking chairs, looking back at what we did, we are able to say, "Thank God for a strong belief in myself. I went for it. I did my best. I have no regrets. Regardless of whether I achieved my goal or not, I went for it. I did the most I could with the most I had. I stepped up to fear. I may be at a different stage of life now and that is what happens to us all. I will never say I lived a life of quiet desperation. And that makes me happy!"

Bottom line: Believe in yourself. Encourage someone today by telling them that you believe in them and watch that little sparkle light up in their eyes. Watch what it does to your own soul. I believe in you. I mean that to the bottom of my toes. If you are reading this, it tells me you are a person just like me on the path to achievement and self-growth. We are all works in progress, and believe me, you are developing what it takes to be what you want to be, do what you want to do, and have what you want to have. I believe in you!

Part Two

The *Elevate* Purpose:
Why are you here?

Chapter Seven:
Recognizing Your Strengths and Priorities

"To be yourself in a world that is constantly trying to make you something else is the greatest accomplishment."

-Ralph Waldo Emerson

The first several chapters have set the foundation for becoming a fully emotionally functioning individual. We focused on: love, character, moral code, forgiveness, acceptance, and belief in ourselves. This has been our foundation for becoming a person of high self-confidence. People with high self-confidence get what they want. Now it is time to explore even more and go into what makes us unique and different. Part Two of this book is about understanding yourself and why you are here. So who the hell are you anyway?

WHO ARE YOU?

Do you know yourself? Have you ever had a numero uno date with yourself and your notepad? Who are you? Really, who are you? This is a fabulous question to ask. A great birthday gift to yourself is to write a one-page bio on you. Who are you right here, right now?

The reason it is so important to explore this is because it gives you your starting point. If you were pushed out of a plane and parachuted into a remote location with one instruction, "You are landing at point A; get to point B." Is it more important for you to know where you are going or know where you are starting? We must know where we are before we can determine what direction we need to go.

You can begin this process by asking yourself the following questions: What are my core values? What is most important to me at this point in my life? What would I die for? What emotions do I experience most of the time? What are my political views? What are my spiritual views? Who are the key relationships in my life? What economic class would I categorize myself in? What are my strengths? What are my areas that need improvement? What are my greatest accomplishments and most embarrassing moments? What do I look like physically? What are my favorite foods, colors, movies, books, games? What do I like to do in my free time? What do I like about myself? What is my personality type?

I challenge you to take the time and ask and answer these questions. When you know yourself, you create certainty which will shine through in everything you do. So let's look at a few of these questions, shall we? The remainder of the chapter will discuss topics that will help define who you are. They will help define what you stand for and why. We are going to dive into core values, priorities, and politics. We will end the chapter by having you determine your personality type and getting clear on whether your passions and skill sets line up with your current career. Let's go!

CORE VALUES:

What are your core values? We focused earlier on character and the solid Big Six: Honesty, Respect, Loyalty, Faith, Courage, and Love. Which ones resonate with you? Which *other* core values resonate with you? If someone asked you what your core values are, could you rattle them off? When we are solid on our core values, it creates the springboard for all of our decisions to be based on. Personally, my top eight core values are: Faith, Love, Courage, Loyalty, Integrity, Balance, Commitment, and Consistency. When I am faced with a big decision, I run them by my core values. For example, when my company was deciding to expand its wellness center locations, I asked myself the preliminary following questions, based on my core values.

Faith: Do I feel that God is leading me in this direction and do I believe it is going to work?

Love: Do I feel that this expansion will provide love to humanity and not harm them in any way?

Courage: Is this expansion causing me a need to become courageous?

Loyalty: Am I being disloyal in any way by expanding my business?

Integrity: Is this vision in line with what I say, think, and do?

Balance: Will this expansion keep me balanced between work and family?

Commitment: Is this something I can commit to with failure not being an option?

Consistency: Will I be able to be consistent with what I need to do to make this expansion successful?

That is one example of how our core values will mold our decisions. Whenever you are making a big decision in your life, run it by your core values. What are your core values and what question have you been asking yourself for a long time but have not yet decided on? "Do I marry this person? Do I take this promotion? Do I begin to exercise again?" Put your question through your core values.

PRIORITIES:

What are your priorities? What is most important to you? I was attending a presentation one time and the speaker said, "Wherever you spend most of your time is what is most important to you." You have probably heard this before, too. At the time, I was twenty-five years old, spending many, many hours growing my chiropractic practice. I was also newly married to my beautiful wife. I was conflicted, thinking that I cared more about my career than my new wife. It affected us both. So naturally, I thought, huh? The speaker went on to make the argument for passive income. You know, work two hours a week and become a millionaire. He went on to say that if you are spending more time at work than with your family, then you must not love your family as much as you love your job. Again, I thought, huh?

Have you heard the statement, conflict equals clarity? Well, after that talk, I got real clear. Folks, we can have *equal* priorities. I repeat, we can have *equal* priorities. I mean, come on, what is most important to you: your right eye or your left eye? They both are!

Some priorities in life are going to take more time than others, depending on what stage of life we are at and what the current situation is at the time. For example, my top priorities are: God, Health, Family, and Wealth. Depending on my current situation these bounce around all of the time in order of time importance. The key is to keep them in continuous balance and understand when one is falling too short or being neglected. Have you heard, whatever you don't respect, you lose? It's a good one to follow. I'm sure you have heard of the classic entrepreneur worth millions who has a divorce to go with each million. You know what they say for entrepreneurs, "Love is grand and divorce is five hundred grand!" It is about keeping them *all* as *equal* priorities.

Depending on your current situation, your time commitment to your priorities will change in order of immediate importance. For example, let's look at different situations you may be in. If you are growing your business, keep your spouse happy! "Honey, I am going to be working late tonight and for the next three Thursdays due to important meetings. Can we change our date night to Friday these next few weeks

67

instead of our regular Thursday?" Did this mean that your job is more important than your spouse? No! They are both important.

"Boss man, my son is playing his championship game this Saturday. Can I get the work done from home and still have it to you by the deadline?" Does this mean that your family is more important than your wealth in this situation? No! They both are important.

We *can* balance out our priorities. You *can* have it all and you *can* get what you want! I'm sure you have heard about the rich man in the hospital bed saying he wished he had spent more time with his family. That is really sad. That is an example of being unbalanced and confused on priorities.

Using my priority examples, God, Health, Family, Wealth, it is all about balance and keeping them *all* important. Don't fall into guilt by not keeping them in this exact priority. Hey, if you are on your deathbed, yes, you can put these in order: God, Health, Family, Wealth. If you are living everyday life, they will bounce around, and with proper communication and proactive planning, it will all work out.

POLITICS:

What are your political views? This is a big part of knowing yourself. Politics usually comes down to economics and morality. I know this is a simplified view. What do you stand for with regards to politics? What party are you or are you not a part of? For me, I understand the basic stereotypical differences between the major political parties and that is about it. I have always felt that most politics are about the golden rule I wrote about earlier, whoever has the most gold, makes the rules. It is all about getting something passed as law and that has a lot to do with cold, hard cash. How else can you explain putting chemicals in our food that are illegal in other countries? Or producing drugs that are given to children that lead to suicidal thoughts? I don't mean to sound pessimistic. I'm an optimist, but come on, look at some of our country's laws. I love America. I love freedom. I would proudly fight for our country if our freedom was under attack. I proudly display the American flag on my front porch. I believe in America. My politics, if you will, come down to personal responsibility. How about you? Where do you stand?

I have pretty much avoided politics up to this point in my life; however it is getting harder to do so. I'm sure you have heard that if you are not part of the solution you are part of the problem. You may have friends that go on and on about political issues to the point of anger, bitterness, and frustration. Many of us watch shows that fuel our political passions. For many of us, politics fuel our human need for significance and certainty. For example, "I am somebody because I have a strong opinion on this topic! I am creating certainty in my life by experiencing the emotion of anger!" For others, this doesn't really apply.

If you are not willing to do something about your political views as far as making positive change, then stop getting so upset.

Here's my take on it, if you are not willing to do something about your political views as far as making positive change, then stop getting so upset. I believe we need to choose our battles. If you are living in frustration because your tax dollars fund abortion clinics, for example, then instead of being irate about it, change it if it is really that important to you. Pour your heart and soul into what you want to see different and politics will become your strength instead of your foe.

We live in the best country in the world. We can do what we want to do when we want to do it. We can be who we want to be in America. I know we have many challenges; however, majority rules, bottom line. As Americans we will never agree on everything. Yes, your tax dollars are going to programs that you do not support. However, the people's tax dollars that you do not support are going to programs that you support and they don't. It all goes in the same pot, and if we don't like where the money is being spent, then get a majority vote and change it. I know this is a simplified view; however, it does come down to majority vote. Do you know a few billionaires that could help you out?

What political party are you? Don't feel you *have* to pick a political party, either. Look, there are great people in all the parties, and I believe, for the most part, they feel they are doing what they think is best. For example, there are good Republicans, Democrats, and Libertarians. There are also bad Republicans, Democrats, and Libertarians. Instead of labeling yourself, look at each political issue and see where you stand independent of the masses.

PERSONALITY:

What is your personality type? Are you more of an extrovert or an introvert? Are you more of a task person or a people person? Are you more formal or informal? Are you more dominant or easy going? Are you more of a producer or a connector? Do you thrive more on steadiness or variety? Are you more motivated by external or internal rewards? We can go on and on. What's great about discovering your personality type is that it lets you know what your personality type is right here, right now. I love personality tests; however, they can be dangerous if you don't see them as a tool to recognize where you are right here, right now. They are not a test to see what personality type you are stuck with for the rest of your life. If you don't like your personality type, change it!

Quite frankly, the best personality type is to be a balance of all of them. If you are a hardcore Type A Driver that hates flexibility, that might not be working for you anymore. If you are a hardcore Type B Supporter that is busy taking care of everyone else except yourself, that might not be working for you anymore, either. Whether it be your horoscope sign, the Chinese zodiac, or a free personality test category you took online, if you don't like what you were categorized in, change it.

Many years ago, my wife and I were sharing a meal with a respected doctor in the community that we both looked up to. We had just learned a simple four-quadrant personality test and shared it with him. Instead of marking which box he was in, he put an x right in the middle of all four quadrants. He was showing us that to be ultimately successful, you need to be all of these personalities. It was a good, "I'll show you the way, grasshopper," moment.

SO WHAT DO YOU WANT TO DO OR BE WHEN YOU GROW UP?

First and foremost, recognize that you were made unique, special, and full of talent. Your job is to shine! Your job is to figure out what your gift is and give it to the world! It can be intimidating at first to have to break down the barriers of not having a belief in yourself or thinking that you are not good enough. Thoughts like, "I'm not good at anything. Who would benefit from what I have to offer?" If you are still thinking this way, it doesn't serve you or anyone else. We all have, or have had, that thought at some point, so recognize that you are not alone. It's a continual process to build ourselves up.

If you are still concerned about what people think, remember to not seek approval from others! Let me help you again with that. Spectators criticize. Those on the sidelines don't have the guts yet to do anything big themselves so they attempt to make themselves feel better by putting others down. It is the classic defeating cycle of low self-esteem. If you know someone like that, give them this book! Many of us are not free until we can get past low self-esteem. So don't care what people think. We are all works in progress.

So what *do* you want to be when you grow up? Have you asked yourself the tough questions? What do I love to do? What am I good at? How can I get paid doing it? These are great questions. If you are not doing something you love, you are not allowing yourself to fully shine. Life really is too short to not do what you deserve to do. If you want to get what you want, it is vital to do the work you love. Once you know what you are good at and how you can serve others with what you are good at, wow, you will be living your full life. For some of us, our career is a good one; however, we are fulfilled performing our passions outside of our career. That is fine, too; just don't hate your job.

Let's look at your current situation. Does your current career line up with your core values? If you work for or run a company, does the company's core values line up with your core values? Is there a challenge to conquer or a need to fulfill? What problem in society really gets you engaged? Most successful companies have a war to win. True passion comes when anger and excitement meet. For example, I am in the wellness industry and the purpose of our company is to change the way our world views health care. Our war is ignorance. We are passionate about telling people the truth about healthy health care instead of following the masses and medicating themselves to death.

Discover what you are passionate about and how you can serve the world with your passion. Continue to ask yourself, "What do I want? How can I make a positive contribution? Does what I want to do match my desired income level? What would I do all day long and not need to get paid for it?"

When beginning to recognize your passions it is helpful to look at your childhood. What did you struggle with as a child? For example, adults who were abused as children may be drawn to help abused children. Adults who were raised in poverty as children may be drawn to a career in finance. Did you have any struggles as a child? This is a big one. Is it possible that you experienced those struggles so that you could relate to others with the same struggle and show them how to overcome it?

I know the question, "What are you passionate about?" can really stump us. It is not an easy answer to rattle off, and it takes some exploration. I am throwing a lot of questions at you to get your mind working on this. Let's tackle this challenge by focusing on these three main questions:

1. What areas of life do you really enjoy? For example, what do you just love: health, finance, animals, sports, children, politics, beauty, fashion, relationships, nature, etc. What areas of life give you your juice?

2. What are your skills and abilities? Take a look at your natural skills and abilities. What am I good at? What do others say I'm good at? What skill or ability do I do that brings me alive? For

example, "I am good at numbers. I am 7 feet tall. I am great with people. I'm a good public speaker. I connect easily. I am really good at checklists. I am super organized."

3. How can you get paid using your skills and abilities in the area of life that you really enjoy? First, ask yourself, "Do I want to be a team member with a great company or do I want to be self-employed? Do I have an entrepreneur mindset or an employee mindset?" If you want to open your own business, ask yourself, "What product or service do people need?" Or if you want to find a great position with an existing company, start with the area of life you enjoy and then make sure your skill sets match up with the job description and make sure you line up with the values of the company.

Take your time with these questions. My wife and I were recently talking about this subject. She is recreating herself, if you will. Both of our boys are in school full time now so she has more time on her hands. We went through the three questions above and came up with this result. She loves middle school aged kids. She also loves self-development. She has tremendous skills and abilities in organization and structure. She thought, okay, what can I do that involves middle school kids and self-development? What can I do that will utilize my skills of structure and organization? What can I do that will combine my passion and my strengths?

She is not in a position where she needs to focus on income so she decided, "I will be a representative for Success for Teens, a non-profit group that helps educate teenagers on self-development concepts! I will mentor teenagers in the school and will be a rock star at it because it lines up perfectly with my passion and strength." So she did just that. She got the program implemented as part of our son's school curriculum and is now starting the program at a second school. This will not only make her extremely happy, it will make a huge impact on making a difference in the world!

Once we know what area of life we enjoy and what skills and abilities we bring to the table, from there it is a matter of bringing it all together. Ask yourself, "What areas of life do I enjoy? What are my skills and abilities? How can I get paid using my skills and abilities in the areas of life that I really enjoy?" Life is a bowl of cherries. Take the biggest bowl you can get!

Bottom line: Know who you are. Know what you value most. Know what you love to do. You were born to let your talents shine. You are not only good enough, you are fabulous, and once you figure out who you are and what your talents are, the world is waiting. God gave you your uniqueness as a gift. He gave you talents as a gift. Your gift back to Him and yourself is what you do with it. It's time to shine, baby.

Elevate

8 Chapter Eight:
Faith and Spirituality

"You gotta have faith!"

-George Michael

So what is faith anyway? What does faith mean? Faith comes from the Greek word "pistis" which literally means to have trust or confidence in someone or something else. I find it ironic that the Greek word "pistis" so closely resembles the slang word pissed, as in "pissed off," which means to urinate or make or become angry. Maybe it's just me that sees the humor in that. Do you get angry or uncomfortable or feel the need to use the restroom when someone starts talking about faith? Hmmm. Let's look at that.

When someone has faith, it means they trust that everything will work out. They know that this too, shall pass. It would be impossible for me to write a book on how to get what you want without including a chapter on faith. Faith is a crucial pillar of self-growth. Faith doesn't have to be spiritual, either. Every time you get in your car for a drive, you are practicing faith that the other drivers do not drive as bad as the person next to you does. Just kidding. But seriously, every time you pass a car coming your way, you are exercising faith that they are not going to come in your lane and hit you head-on. Every time you send your kids to school, you are practicing faith that a highly disturbed individual has not been prescribed mind-altering medication and is going to show up with a shotgun. Faith is crucial to live the *Elevate* lifestyle. George Michael got it right when he sang, "You gotta have faith!"

So why is faith important? Well, spiritually speaking, when you know God believes in you, it enables you to have a stronger faith in your ability to accomplish what you set out to accomplish. It's been said that if we have the faith of a mustard seed, we can move mountains. I believe this to be metaphorical, but hey, you never know. Faith helps us push through the mountains of challenges that will come our way. When we have faith that God has our back and is *for us*, just watch how much strength that gives you to accomplish what you want.

As a human race, we value the power of life. This is a form of faith. There is something innate inside of us that appreciates life. I was walking into work recently and I passed a very pregnant woman. I'm talking ready to pop pregnant. I smiled at her with a warm smile. As I walked passed her, I wasn't sure why I smiled, and then I realized there is something remarkable about a growing baby inside of her. Of course there is also something remarkable about a woman that carries a baby for nine months, too! There is something remarkable about life. As a society we come together to protect innocent life. For example, if you have ever seen someone choke in public or have a heart attack, society stops. We move in to help. When innocent life is being lost, we come together. This is faith.

RELIGION

As we discuss faith, don't get spiritual faith mixed up with religion. Religion is a specific set of spiritual beliefs that a specific group follows based on culture and belief systems. It is a personal or institutionalized system grounded in belief of the super natural. Religion can be extremely beneficial, and it can also be extremely destructive. We all know how divisive religion is, and it just doesn't need to be. I hope at the same time that we all also know of religious families, for example, that are wonderful and not at all divisive.

Religion is a specific set of spiritual beliefs that a specific group follows based on culture and belief systems.

Person A needs to respect Person B, regardless of what they believe or practice spiritually. Just like in the Moral Code chapter, if we are not harming ourselves or others physically or mentally, then let people believe what they want to believe. If you want, you can be an example and show them your way, but your way may not be their way. I can assure you that their soul does not rest in your hands. That is between them and God.

Sometimes religion gets a bad rap because the stance is taken by some religious groups that they are the only way or they are the only ones that have it right. I know this is a touchy topic and can be fiercely defended. If you study all of the major religions, although they are different in many ways, they are also very much alike in many ways. One of the biggest differences in them is what happens after we die.

And unless you have come back from the dead, this one will not be answered with total certainty.

So knowing there are many differences, let's step back and take a look at the big picture of religion; it's Love. That is the big picture. For example, when Jesus was asked what the number one and two most important commandments were, he said love God with all of your heart and love your neighbor as yourself. Isn't that the big picture? Love God and your fellow man. The big picture is about respecting each other, loving each other, helping each other, and coming together as a community. There is only one source of life, regardless of what we call it, how we practice it, or how we have a relationship with it. I have many friends in different religions, and they all get their prayers answered, and they all live by a great set of values, and they all are the most grounded people I know.

So with religion aside, I am going to continue this chapter assuming that you believe in a creator, a source of all energy and life; the same source that makes your heart beat, a flower bloom, and the Earth rotate. If you are still feeling blocked by the term "God", please continue to read with an open mind. For some of us, we hear the word God, and all rational intelligence goes out the door. Personally for me, I have struggled in many ways seeking out the truth and certainty of my own spiritual beliefs. I will share more about this later. For now, look at God as your creator. Look at God as your source of the ultimate: Unconditional Love, Strength, Wisdom, Encouragement, Security, Guidance, Peace, and Understanding.

SPIRITUAL FAITH

Spiritual faith comes down to whether we were created by an intelligent designer or not. If you don't believe there is a creator, keep reading. You may have heard the argument of intelligent design. Is there an intelligence that designed us? Is there a creator? I am in no way prepared to discuss creation versus evolution and the intricacies of single cell mutation and Darwinism. I do find it interesting though that even though Charles Darwin had some great answers, he did not have an answer on the *source of the creation* of the single cell. He did prove that there was evidence of an intelligent designer though.

Whether we came from a big bang, rocks colliding, a spark from gas, apes, Adam and Eve, or even aliens, something created all of it. The way we were created has never been as important to me as the idea of an actual creator causing it all. It's the old question, what came first the chicken or the egg? Something created the chicken or the egg. Something created the first cell. Something created a monkey, something created a rock, something created a spark, and something may have even created aliens.

If you want to really dive into this argument, search online "Proof of God" and then search for "Proof of Atheism." I think if both sides realized that there is too much organization in life to have been started by an accident and that the world was not literally flooded only sparing two animals of each species, then both the atheists and creationists could come together and experience what God represents, regardless of how it all started. I think ignorance needs to be recognized on both sides. The choice is yours. For me, if I didn't believe in my creator, I would be very challenged by what my purpose was. If I came from a spark from two rocks or an explosion of gas, then for what the hell reason do I exist? If there is no purpose, what is the purpose? For me, my spiritual faith is grounded in knowing that I was born for a purpose. I was born with gifts to share with the world. I was born to love others as God loves me. As I said above, for me, God is my total source of the ultimate: Unconditional Love, Strength, Wisdom, Encouragement, Security, Guidance, Peace, and Understanding. It is my belief that everyone wants this in their life.

For me, it is all about the magnificence of life, and I simply cannot conceive our creation being by chance. Let's start with the universe. I personally enjoy the statistics of intelligent design. For example, there is a 10 to the 21st power chance that the force of the Big Bang could have randomly been properly balanced with the mass and gravity of the universe in order for the stars and planets to form, so that life could exist here in our cosmos.[7] That is 10 to the 21st power! That is a big number—1,000,000,000,000,000,000,000. Just as a comparison, the number one billion looks like this—1,000,000,000. One billion minutes ago was the year 108! Wow!

Did you know that the Earth rotates at a speed of 1100 mph on a 23.5 degree axial tilt? This speed and tilt is perfect for our planet's survival. The Earth is 92,960,000 miles from the sun. A minor decrease in the sun's distance would cause a major heating effect on the Earth's surface, eventually killing us all.

Did you know that when a sperm and egg come together, they form a 72 trillion-cell baby? Did you know that electrical impulses travel through our nervous system at 180,000 mph? Did you know that a watermelon starts out as a seed and grows to 200,000 times its weight from dirt, water and sun? I like to think that we have a grand designer. I cannot fathom the idea of not having a designer when I witness, on a daily basis, such incredible, miraculous organization.

It gets tricky when people ask what God's name is. How do I know He loves me? Where is God now? How can bad things happen to good people? There are multitudes of answers out there, and some may work for you, and some may not. Some we will never know. Don't let the not knowing part rob you from faith. I don't believe that anyone can prove their answer is the right one. Sometimes we can create certainty in this area by accepting the fact that we will never know until we meet our creator. The following are *my* answers that have rested *my* soul.

WHAT IS GOD'S NAME?

Whatever you call him. God is the creator of the world. I think He is bigger than a title.

HOW DO I KNOW HE LOVES ME?

Look at the organization of your human body. Search online for cellular biology or the endocrine system, for example. You were made with incredible organization. Why would God create you with such miraculous design if He didn't want you to shine? Why would God create your body that can self-heal and self-regulate if He didn't want you to survive? Every time your body shivers when you are cold, your innate intelligence is creating warmth to get your body back to 98.6 degrees! That is God's love. You were created. That alone is a sign of love. When you feel God's guidance or get a strong intuition to avoid a bad circumstance, that is God's love. That is your proof to see that He wants what is best for you. That is love. Have you had that little voice inside you that says, "Don't do that, it will destroy your life?" Where did that voice come from? When a walking baby stands over the stairs, the baby does not walk off of the stairs, regardless if you told them not to. That was already inside of them. That is God's love. When a Mama bear cuddles and nurtures a baby cub, that is sign of God's love. If God did not love us, why would He even put the emotion of love into us? I believe love is the highest form of bliss, and He wants us to experience that.

I was walking downtown one day, and a guy came up to me out of nowhere and started talking to me as we were walking. I was headed to lunch and I didn't even make eye contact with him until he started talking to me. He told me he had just gone into a convenience store, drank half a bottle of Gatorade, and put it back on the shelf. He then said that he yelled at the clerk and told her to go ahead and call the cops, *that* he was *not* afraid to go back to jail. He then proceeded to tell me that he is going to get five dollars and go back and throw it in her face and show her who "the man" is. He then told me he was a cook on his way to cook meth at a lab. He told me all of the ingredients and where to get them. I wasn't really sure what to say other than have a nice day. I was too much in shock to say much more.

What does this have to do about God's love for us? The day before this happened we shot videos for Chapter One: Love. The following week we were going to shoot videos on Chapter Two: Character. My mind was working on what kind of video we can shoot for the character chapter. The experience I had with this meth guy came one day after shooting videos on love and one week prior to shooting videos on character. This experience showed me that God was present with me. It showed me that people need the message of this book and encouraged me to keep on moving forward with it. He showed me that the world needs *Elevate*. That was God's love.

WHERE IS GOD NOW?

In you, in me, in all things. He is in everything. It is our job to let Him out. It is our job to experience His source of: Unconditional Love, Strength, Wisdom, Encouragement, Security, Guidance, Peace, and Understanding. We are God's hands and feet. We can be part of that or we can choose not to. I want to clarify that I do not believe that we are God. I do not believe that we are the source and creator of the universe or the source or creator of our individual universe. However, we can direct our lives the way we want by our choices and create the life we want. Understanding this, we still are completely out of control of others' actions, choices, or natural disasters. I believe the biggest thing to focus on with this question is that God lives within each of us, and that we can express His unconditional love toward others.

I love the story about the man who was on top of his rooftop during a flood. He prays to God, "God, please come save me!" A few hours later, some people in a boat come by and ask him to get in. He says, "No thanks, God is going to save me." A few more hours go by and a pilot in a helicopter comes by with a rope and asks him to climb the rope and get on the helicopter. He says, "No thanks, God is going to save me." A few hours later, he drowns. He goes to Heaven and asks God, "Why didn't you save me?" God says, "Really? I sent two men in a boat. I sent a pilot in a helicopter. I did come to save you!" Look, we are God's hands and feet. While I do believe in miracles, I also believe that we are greatly used to deliver God's love to the world.

HOW CAN BAD THINGS HAPPEN TO GOOD PEOPLE?

Let me start by categorizing this question into three parts. One, was it really a bad thing? Two, was I, or someone else, personally responsible for it? And, three, was it truly something that happened that was beyond personal responsibility?

First, was it really a bad thing? We need to clarify if the situation that happened or is happening is truly "bad." Maybe it is going to be "good" in the long run. Look at everything in your life that was interpreted as "bad" and ask yourself how has it served you now? This may blow your mind. For example, "If I didn't get laid off, I would have never started my now successful business." Most "bad" situations, even though we may not have understood it at the time, greatly turned out to be "good" for us down the road. Your adversity becomes your strength. A muscle needs to be torn to grow. Things happen to us to serve us in the long run. This is where we do not always understand God's wisdom, but if you trust that His wisdom will be revealed, "bad" situations can be our greatest strength.

Second, was I, or someone else, personally responsible for it? God does not control our personal choices or the personal choices of others. That is why wrong things can happen. When someone does the Bad Six: Lies, Cheats, Steals, Mentally Harms, Physically Destroys, or Physically Abuses another or themselves, this is wrong. God did not control that. That was a personal choice of someone else. If you were killed by a murderer, and you were a good person, God does not control the wrong actions of others. This is big. "How could God allow those innocent people to get shot by that mad man?" God does not control the personal choice of the mad man. God gave us the gift of personal responsibility. It will be abused as long as we shall live.

God does not control the wrong actions of others.

If we really dive deep into this, we may be surprised about some of the personal choices we are making that we are not even aware of. For example, a smoker may say, "How could God let me get emphysema?" God had nothing to do with it. The smoker made the personal choice to take the risk of destroying their lungs, whether they knew it was going to kill them or not. This is like someone who has not broken out of the poverty mentality saying, "How could God let me be poor?" Have you read a book on wealth? Do you save ten percent? "How could our house burn down?" Is it possible that the electrical work was shady? What did God have to do with that?

As a doctor, I hear this regarding diseases a lot. "How could God let me get this?" Look, I am very sensitive to this. Just because we take personal responsibility does not mean it is this clear-cut. It is vital to meet people where they are at, show compassion, and show them a better way, if they are willing. Most diseases have causes. Just because we do not know the cause, does not mean there is not a cause. For example, cancer, in most cases, was caused by a cancer-causing agent. Most of our diseases in our current society are from lifestyle. Most diseases stem from toxicity or deficiency. They are from loss of function. If you *really* want to find out what may have *caused* the disease, you need to seek out the answer from different sources.

Third, was this "bad" event that happened truly beyond personal responsibility? These are the events in life that were not caused by another human. Let's take natural disasters for example, earthquakes, floods, etc. How do we not know that it had to happen ultimately for the survival of the Earth? For example, did you know that forest fires caused by lightning are necessary for the forest to regenerate? I do know that our planet survives just as our human body does. The only answer that I can rest on in this rare category is that I do not know the "why" of everything. I can only trust that it will ultimately turn out for the good.

GOOD VERSUS EVIL

This can get pretty heated for many of us. No pun intended. I really dove into good versus bad and right versus wrong in the Moral Code chapter. There is very much a right and a wrong. Good and bad is how we interpret it. But how do we explain evil? Is there really a devil in a red suit with two horns and a pitchfork that lives in the center of the fiery Earth? This image was created in the medieval times, by the way. So dismissing the fictional character, is there a force whose job is to steal, kill, and destroy? This can't be ignored as we watch the evening news tonight, again!

Let's look at evil in the form of temptation. Have you heard God is everywhere, so how can evil exist if God is everywhere? Whether we believe that good and evil are from the same source or from two different sources doesn't change the fact that God allows it. What if God loves us enough to give us personal choice and responsibility? So with regards to temptation, regardless of where it comes from, it is real, and if you want to get what you want, my suggestion is that you do not pretend that it does not exist.

Every day we have choices to make that can get us closer to our destiny or take us far from it. Call it evil, call it wrong, or call it a poor choice, every day we are faced with temptation that when acted upon, or ignored, will determine the direction of our life. Ill-intentioned temptation when acted upon may lead to death, disease, prison, divorce, etc. If you are tempted to rob a bank, it may cost you your life. If you are tempted to have unprotected sex with someone you just met, it may cause you a disease. If you are tempted to physically harm another human being, it may lead to prison. If you are tempted to commit adultery, it may cost you your family. Folks, temptation has a source. It stems from: hate, guilt, inadequacy, depression, greed, power, and lust. That is what I call evil. I don't have the complete answer of where it comes from, but I do know it is real and that we need to recognize that it is real so we can be prepared and stand guard against it. I hope that the first few chapters of this book will help us find the source of any: hate, guilt, inadequacy, depression, greed, power, or lust that we may be struggling with.

I understand that sometimes we need to experience "bad" things to recognize what is "good," and sometimes "good" things do come out of "bad" things; however, if we can be proactive from the start, I don't believe we *have* to experience "bad" in order to experience "good."

MY PERSONAL SPIRITUAL CHALLENGES

I am including this section in hopes that some of you may relate. There are answers to your questions. Keep seeking your truth because we all deserve certainty in this area. I personally consider myself an open-minded, explorative, answer-seeking Christian. I became a Christian twenty-five years ago. I started as a non-practicing Catholic. My extended family was Catholic, but we never went to church, and I didn't know anything about Catholicism. My mom and I became Pentecostal Christians when I was a teenager. There, my spiritual walk was spent combating the devil, experiencing the Holy Spirit, and focusing on right and wrong. It served me well for the time I was involved. Then I moved into the Non-denominational Christian realm, where I really experienced more of a personal relationship with God through music, prayer, love, and grace. Non-denominational Christianity really showed me how to put my faith into action by loving God and helping others.

And then I wanted more answers. For me, I knew I was missing something. I then began to seek out some of the new-age beliefs and eastern religions. Why would I ignore all of the other great spiritual leaders that were around hundreds and thousands of years before

Jesus Christ? Those teachings have given me great insight into my spiritual walk that I did not get from the Bible alone. I didn't line up with all of it; however, a lot of it I did.

This book is a contemplation of self-leadership, emotional intelligence, and spirituality. It is the result of my inquisitive personality always seeking truth. What are the answers? You are now reading many of them. This book truly helps you get what you want, and what you want is really *true happiness*.

So if you are in the same boat as I was, let's look at some more answers that have settled my spirit. You may or may not agree. The purpose of me sharing my answers is to give you perspective that may be similar or may be different from your own. I can promise you that whatever you believe, I will respect. These are my current answers, and at the same time, I am committed to lifetime learning. When we stop learning, we stop living.

THE BIBLE

I have had some major challenges with the fundamental interpretation of scripture. I was greatly challenged by the teachings regarding original sin, heaven and hell, the major difference between the Old and New Testament, and lastly, the relevance of the cultural teachings of the biblical times as it stands today in our culture. When I asked my questions, I was told that the Bible is the inspired Word of God and that Jesus is either one hundred percent correct or Jesus was crazy and we should ignore everything He said. This answer didn't work for me anymore. Perhaps Jesus was greatly misunderstood. Look at some of the interpretations we use in our society today. Is it possible that the teachings of Jesus have been greatly misinterpreted?

As an emerging Christian, I believe the Bible needs to be read symbolically *and* literally. Scripture depends on the specific group of people that were being addressed at the time and what their challenges were. I don't think Jesus really wants me to pluck out my eyes or cut off my hands, for example. After reading the New Testament three times, I couldn't imagine it any other way. Some parts are metaphorical and some parts are historical. Some are relevant to us here and now and some are not relevant to us here and now. Some parts tell us what to do and some parts described what they did at that time. When I took this perspective and read it again, it really started to line up for me.

It is dangerous to accept *any* teaching with complete blind faith. As soon as we ignore our rational thought it can lead to totally unethical behavior and literal insanity. I touched on rules and society briefly in the Moral Code chapter. When teachings go against the Bad Six: Lie, Cheat, Steal, Mentally Harm, Physically Destroy, or Physical Abuse, we need to completely reverse the interpretation as it stands for us now in our current society. Christians, for example were considered good Christians during the Crusades, 1096 AD - 1272 AD, as they killed hundreds of thousands of people that were not of the same faith. Women and children were killed in the name of God. We can look back nearly a thousand years ago now and say, what were they thinking? That is crazy. To them though, they were following the inspired leaders of God. They were following the interpretation of the Bible at that time. They were blindly following leaders that were grossly misinterpreting the Bible and abusing their power. Some people still beat their children, still look at women as inferior, and still believe in slavery, all based on their interpretation of the Bible. Folks, that's crazy. This is the same radical kind of thought that fuels terrorism based on the interpretation of the Koran.

There are many different ways to interpret the teachings in the Bible. Look at how many different Christian religions there are. It is our job to rationally choose an interpretation that follows the number one and number two rules of Jesus, which as you know, is to love God and treat others how you want to be treated. The Bible is a wonderful source of inspiration, logic, guidelines, stories, examples, and truth. How we interpret it is what has so many Bible followers lost in the battle of blind faith versus rational thought.

HEAVEN/HELL

My biggest challenge in my spiritual path was a belief in hell as a physical location. As author Brian McLaren points out, most major religions have some sort of hell. Fundamental Christianity describes hell. Orthodox Jews retain the concept of hell. The Koran describes seven layers of hell. Hinduism describes twenty-one hells. Classic Buddhism has seven hells and Tibetan Buddhism has eight hells. What the hell?

I have a good friend that is a Buddhist and he comes from a great family. His great grandfather was Buddhist, his grandfather was Buddhist, his father was Buddhist, and now he is Buddhist. That is all he knows and it has worked for him. I remember getting into a debate with a Christian friend saying, "How can he go to hell just because he does not know Jesus?" If a Christian missionary offered him the gift of salvation through Jesus Christ and he politely said, "No thank you. I love my culture. I love my God, and I love my rituals. My prayers are answered, and I already live in a state of peace and understanding."

Well guess what, he gets to burn in hell now because he didn't accept Jesus? Isn't God bigger than this? Why would he have even been created if God knew he was not going to choose Jesus? That doesn't make sense. Yes, we have free will to make choices, but why would he have even been born as God's creation in the first place?

I am certainly not a biblical scholar; this is my understanding of what the truth is as far as I understand it. I believe God's message of Heaven and Hell can be interpreted as the Heaven and Hell we create by our choices here and now. Did you know that the word hell comes from the Greek word "Gehenna?" "Ge" means valley and "Henna" means Hinnom. The word Gehenna literally means Valley of Hinnom. Did you know that the Valley of Hinnom was where the city dump was just outside Jerusalem? Yeah! That's what I said. When Jesus talked about hell, in that culture at that time, he was referring to the city dump where there was garbage, waste, constant fire, and weeping wild animals gnashing their teeth as they fought! The more I dive into the biblical scholars' interpretation of hell, it is very, very evident that it is very uncertain and can be interpreted *many* ways.

Did you know that the Kingdom of God or Kingdom of Heaven can be interpreted as "loving God and others" here and now? Did you know that salvation can be interpreted as "love and compassion" and "to be protected from harm?"

These answers blew my mind and made me proud to be a follower of Jesus again. He was all about love and helping people. These answers got me back to His number one and two commandments: Love God with all of our heart and treat others how we want to be treated. For me, Jesus Christ works. He came in the flesh and experienced life like we do. He is my ultimate example of how to live. He is my savior. He is my God. That is *my* personal path.

Heaven can be here now. Hell can be here now! What happens after we die, I do not know for certain. My heaven right here, right now, is making a difference, loving God, being my best, and helping others. I do believe that once we pass, our choices we made in life will be reviewed and we will be reunited with our loved ones that have passed before us. Maybe we can hang out, maybe we can come down as angels, and maybe we can come back for another round. Only God knows.

As I have said before, I am far from a Bible scholar and I know my answers may stir up some debate. What I am certain of is that I am finding my truth and this works for me. If we were to define Heaven in terms of emotions here and now they would be: unconditional love, acceptance, forgiveness, belief, faith, purpose, strength, joy, inspiration, positivity, happiness, security, guidance, peace, understanding, and servanthood. If we were to define Hell in terms of emotions here and now, they would be: hate, non-acceptance of self, resentment, worry, anxiety, no purpose, weakness, inadequacy, depression, judgment, criticalness, negativity, selfishness, emptiness, solitude, and victimhood.

Continue to seek out your truth. A huge part of knowing yourself is being certain on what you believe spiritually. Take the time to get certain on what you believe and why.

> **Bottom line:** You deserve to know that everything is going to be okay. Have trust and confidence that your path is revealing itself. You deserve to know your own spiritual truths. You deserve to experience faith and spirituality. A tremendous part of getting what you want is having faith and a relationship with your creator.

Elevate

Chapter Nine:
The Purpose of Life

"I am here for a purpose and that purpose is to grow into a mountain, not to shrink to a grain of sand. Henceforth, will I apply ALL my efforts to become the highest mountain of all and I will strain my potential until it cries for mercy."

-Og Mandino

As I write this chapter on the purpose of life, my dad is probably going to die tonight. I wish I was kidding. He was getting ready to turn seventy-five years old this month, and he's definitely not going to make it another three weeks to his birthday. As we speak, his bed is set up in the living room, and my mom and hospice are keeping him comfortably medicated as cancer takes his last breathe. He was diagnosed with bladder cancer a couple of months ago. My dad, whom I affectionately call "Pops," came into my life at the age of twelve. He was my dad that taught me how to tie a tie, how to have a great sense of humor, how to stand up for myself, how to choose good friends, how to fish with two hooks, and how to be kind to others. When he came into my life, I was shown what a family with stability looked like. I will forever be grateful for my relationship with my Pops for all of these years.

I think the hardest part about his passing is his attitude of perseverance. He still has not accepted the fact that he is dying. He is still positive, has his sense of humor, and is still hoping for a miracle. As it has gotten extremely difficult to understand him when he talks, I am proud to say that he never gave up all the way to the end. He wanted me to make sure my sons and his grandsons knew that you never quit! Keep going! Never give up. Pops, I love you and I promise you that as your grandsons get older and read this chapter, they will know what an incredible person you were to them, to me, and to all those who loved you.

Ronald Hiett 1938-2013

So what if this life was all there was? What if death was the end? What is the purpose of waking up every day? Why am I here? I believe that we all have these challenging questions at some point in our lives. What is the purpose of life? This is *the* question. What is the purpose of life? Is it to find love? Is it to raise children? Is it to become financially rich? What is it for you? It means many different things to many different people. For some it means to be successful in everything they do. To others it means to help as many people as possible with the gifts and talents they have been given. For some it means to reach a spiritual plateau of peace and understanding. What is the purpose of life? It is a gigantic question and when answered, it brings an incredible amount of clarity and vision. The purpose of life, yes, folks, it's a big one.

I have the answer. Are you ready? Drum roll please... The purpose of life is to Love God, Be Your Best and Help Others. Tadaaaa! That's it! The purpose! That's why you were born, my friend. The purpose of life is to Love God, Be Your Best and Help Others.

LOVE GOD

Let's start with loving God, love your creator. We explored loving God in chapter one. The reason it was in chapter one is because loving God is the most important thing you could ever do to get what you want. How is that working for you? How do you experience God? To love God means to stay connected with your creator, to stay connected with the source of life. It is the most important relationship you have. This is the relationship that reminds you to practice unconditional love toward yourself and others. Love God. I'm assuming we have reached agreement that our definition of God equates to love. How about you start with these examples:

> *To love God means to stay connected with your creator, to stay connected with the source of life.*

Hug others—When we express and receive love toward another human being, we are loving God. Did you know that when a child is raised with hugs, the part of their brain that is responsible for learning, memorizing, and responding to stress, grows ten percent bigger![8]

Prayer and meditation—When we settle into the stillness of our minds, we are loving God. Have you ever tried to quiet your mind for even three minutes? Give it a shot. There is a reason meditation is so beneficial. When you are silent with God, like He was sitting right next to you, you are loving God.

Listen to your goose bumps—When we listen to inspirational music and get overwhelmed with an incredible feeling of joy, we are loving God. When we follow that inspirational voice inside and do what we are afraid to do, we are loving God.

Get in awe—Getting in awe is about gratefulness. When we watch a beautiful sunrise or look at the ocean or mountain range, we are loving God. When we witness the miracle of a child's birth, we are loving God. When we study the supreme organization of our body's physiology or our world, we are loving God.

How do you love God? I believe one of the main purposes of life is to love God. I remember a little girl walking up to my wife and giving her a flower many years ago. It happened to her again at a coffee shop last year. These little girls were loving God by showing another person unconditional love. Begin today. Follow this purpose for your life. Be sure to experience more of: Unconditional Love, Strength, Wisdom, Encouragement, Security, Guidance, Peace, and Understanding.

BE YOUR BEST

Next, be your best! The main recipe I know of for emotional disaster is to not become what you know you are capable of. Whatever you can be, you must be. Believe in yourself. You can be what you want to be. Break those shackles of inhibition and go after what you want. Aren't you happiest when you're growing, accomplishing something, or going after what is important to you? Look, if there is any fear or victimhood, take responsibility for your life. It can start over now. If you fall down, get back up. Keep moving forward. You are worth it. Be your best.

Have you ever been asked to imagine the world without you in it? This question can kind of sting. For example, do you know much about your great grandfather? I don't. I know my great grandfather came from Hungary and had his own business. I'm glad he did, that's for sure. What are *our* great grandkids going to say about our legacy? Are you making a difference? Are you focused on thriving or are you just surviving? Folks, this life is our shot. Be your best!

I think the question, "How would the world be much different if you were not in it," can be very revealing. For one, it tests your purpose. It is a gut check into how we are showing up and affecting the person in the mirror every day. It is a gut check on our so-called "problems." I think this question can stimulate us to be our best and help us to not let things bother us so much.

Have you heard the philosophy, you are not your thoughts? *My* take on this is that you are *more* than just your thoughts. You are a shining light in this world. You do matter! Your opinions matter! Your unique personality matters! You must shine your light. You can make a difference. You have the same power in you that is in the Sun! Let your light shine, baby! Your existence matters! You matter!

HELP OTHERS

Next, help others. It is easy to get overwhelmed by all the people and all the movements and all the causes that ask for and need our help. Don't get jaded. Apathy is your enemy, remember? Care, and care deeply for others. Choose your cause and get active. I definitely follow the philosophy that most often, the helping hand we need is at the end of our own arms. However, this does not mean we don't sometimes need a push.

Help others who want to help themselves and/or who cannot physically help themselves. If you are busy helping others that have no desire to help themselves, it might make you feel better at the end of the day, but in the big picture of life, not much of a difference is being made. I will leave you to interpret when helping others is *truly* helping others or is actually *enabling* others. For example, you will rarely see me give money to the person on the street corner with a sign that says, *Will Work For Food.* Talk to those guys sometime. In most cases, they really won't work for food, or *even* work for money. In most cases, they are *already* working for money by standing on that corner asking for handouts, and you just entered their storefront. You are now the customer. Even the Bible says that if you don't work, you don't eat. Check out some of our interviews with the homeless at www.Elevate Book.com/Bonus

Remember, we all need help at times. Help people who cannot help themselves *and* help people who are willing to help themselves. Who can you help today? Have you heard the story about the starfish on the beach?

A grandfather was walking with his grandson early one morning and thousands of starfish were swept up on the shore from the high tide earlier that morning. The grandson began to pick up as many starfish as he could and throw them back into the ocean. The grandfather chuckled and said, "Do you really think you are going to make a difference? There are thousands of them! You will never be able to save them all!" The grandson picked up another one, showed his grandfather and threw it into the ocean. The grandson said, "I may not be able to help all of these starfish, but I sure made a difference to that one."

Bottom line: The secret to life, the purpose, is to Love God, Be Your Best, and Help Others. Put it all together to find the way this purpose fits into your unique purpose. Take action and live your purpose deliberately.

Elevate

Part Three:
The *Elevate* Mindset
How to Think Well

Elevate

10 Chapter Ten:
Choice and Responsibility

"You cannot escape the responsibility of tomorrow by evading it today."

-Abraham Lincoln

Part Three of Elevate is all about your mindset. Do you know how to think to get what you want? What a great question. Do you know why you think the way you do regarding the various areas of your life including: love, marriage, children, money, friendships, and health? Most of us are programmed from our families and other childhood influences to think the same way that *they* think. It is up to us to ask ourselves if that level of thinking is working for us or not. It is up to us to look at each category in our life and ask ourselves if we are happy with the results. If we are not, then we must determine what we believe in these areas and ask ourselves if we want to continue believing that way or not. Regardless of how we were programmed, it is now our choice to determine if how we think is helping us or hurting us to get what we want.

YOU WERE BRAINWASHED

Let's look at a few categories: God, Health, Family, and Wealth. Were you taught that God loves you? Keep thinking that way. God's love has served as your source to love yourself and others. Were you taught that God is here to punish you? Stop thinking that way. It doesn't serve you. Assess each of these areas and ask yourself if you are getting what you want from each area. Were you taught that we are all going to die from something so don't worry about your health? Well, that statement is true if you don't mind cutting your quality and quantity of life by thirty years or so. Were you taught that your body is your gift and your vehicle for life and should be treated extremely well? If you were, you are probably very fit, energetic, and express a high level of vitality. Were you taught that family isn't that important and when things go wrong you leave? That doesn't work, does it? Were you taught that families are worth pushing through the challenges to make the family unit stronger? I bet you have a great loving family if you were taught that program. Were you taught that money is bad and you shouldn't care about it? If you are still operating in that program, my guess is that you struggle financially. Again, you get the point.

It is our responsibility to ask ourselves why we think the way we do. Who programmed our mind? Where did my current level of thought come from and is it still working for me? If it is not, then hot damn, today is your lucky day because you now have the freedom to think the way you want to think. You now have the freedom to program your mind in a way that helps you, not hinders you. You now have the freedom to choose to think in a way that gives you the opportunity to get what you want.

GUARD YOUR INFLUENCES

Do you only take advice from people you want to be like? This can be a big one if you answered no. If you take advice from people that you *do not* want to be like, you begin to think the way they think and have what they have. Only, only, only take advice from people that you *want* to be like. If you don't, many times, especially when someone is giving you unsolicited advice, they are trying to convince themselves about a decision they have made as they are giving their advice to you. If you want to be rich, take advice from someone who is rich. If you want to be healthy, take advice from someone that is healthy. If you want marriage advice, take advice from a couple who have a great marriage. You get the point.

If you find yourself around others who are making decisions and choices that no longer line up with who you are or who you are becoming, make the choice to eliminate or greatly decrease your exposure to them.

The people in your life are extremely influential to your future. Make sure they are encouraging you, putting courage in you, and not discouraging you, taking courage out of you. If you find yourself around others who are making decisions and choices that no longer line up with who you are or who you are becoming, make the choice to eliminate or greatly decrease your exposure to them. You really do become like the people you hang out with.

If you are ever around someone who starts to belittle your ambitions, recognize that only small people do that and life is too short to be little, remember? Give them this book and run for your life. I'm not kidding. Some people can help us get what we want and some people can shoot us down and try to prevent us from getting what we want. Be on guard.

GUARD YOUR THOUGHTS

You must guard your thoughts to get what you want. Your mind is hungry. Your mind goes after whatever stimulus you put in front of it. Garbage in really does equal garbage out! If we feed our minds with negative news, conversations, people, and music, our output becomes negative. My dad always told me, "If you want to soar with the eagles, you cannot hang out with turkeys." Surround yourself with people and experiences that make you feel good about yourself. You will never outperform the expectations of those you hang out with.

How do you show up to other people? Do others feel good about themselves after talking to *you*? If we don't consciously choose what goes in our mind we are losing. Many of us are grumpy, exhausted, and broke. Many of us are this way because we allow others that are struggling with the same things to confirm with us that this is what life is all about. We allow our minds to continually get programmed that this is normal. We soon become fine with being average. Once we are fine with being average, complacency sets in. Complacency is a lot like apathy. It is extremely dangerous. Bind it and get it out of your life, like NOW!

The reason we need to guard our thoughts with incredible vigor is because our minds tend to take the path of our most common repetitive thoughts. Our minds get lazy and continue to think the way we always think. Based on the thoughts we have most of the time, neural pathways in our brain literally get stronger. When you think a certain way consistently, that thought pathway becomes the path of least resistance for more of the same thoughts.

For example, when we spend time with negative thoughts like: destruction, inadequacy, weakness, hurt, anger, and frustration; this tells our minds to hang out there more often. Conversely, when we spend time with positive thoughts like: joy, love, proactive-ness, abundance, strength, and happiness; this tells our minds to hang out *there* more often.

Never let a negative sentence get completed in our heads. The moment you feel yourself beginning to think about negative thoughts, say "STOP" or "CANCEL," and move on to your next thought. The negative thoughts will fade and leave room for the positive ones. A beautiful flower garden is only a beautiful flower garden when we regularly pull out the weeds.

WINNER VERSUS WEENIE

We have the power of choice to choose which thoughts we have! Our thoughts become our feelings. Our feelings become our actions. Our actions become the results in our life. Please read those again. Do you listen to the winner thoughts or the weenie thoughts? If you don't know the difference, begin to monitor your thoughts, and if they are taking you away from the vision you have for your life, then stop thinking that way. If your thoughts move you closer to the vision you have for your life, then keep thinking that way. What happens in our lives is usually a result of the things we constantly think about.

Picture a little weenie and a little winner competing in your mind. I know, I know, get creative. They both are really hungry and they like to fight with each other. The little winner represents happiness, which is: joy, love, serenity, kindness, compassion, truth, and generosity. The little weenie represents unhappiness, which is: fear, anger, worry, jealousy, sorrow, inferiority, self-pity, and resentment. Although they fight all the time, the one that wins is the one that you feed most. Do any of us need to go on a starvation plan?

Weenie Thoughts	Winner Thoughts
Fear of failure	Confidence to learn from mistakes
Fear of success	Acceptance of high self-worth
Seeking approval from others	Seeking approval from self
Have to do something	*Get* to do something
Lack/Scarcity	Abundance of opportunity
Blame others	Accept responsibility
Knowing from intellect only	Knowing from results only
See challenges as problems	See problems as challenges

THE POWER OF CONTROL

I know for some of us, life can be tough. Really, life can kick us down at times. Continue to work on yourself, be tough on yourself. When you are tough on yourself, life will become easier. We must take one hundred percent responsibility for our lives in order to get what we want. Taking one hundred percent responsibility means we can no longer play the blame game. It doesn't work, and it robs you of your ability to make things better. How can you make things better if you blame? It is impossible. One hundred percent responsibility means that we can no longer live our lives as if someone is coming to bail us out.

You are in control. No one is coming to save your marriage; no one is coming to save your finances; no one is coming to save your relationship with your children; and no one is coming to save your health. One hundred percent responsibility means that you are always asking yourself the question, "What am I doing to cause this situation or grief in my life?" This is a life-changing question. Put this one on your bathroom mirror. Once you answer it, ask yourself, "What am I going to do about it?" Recognize the areas of your life that you are not happy with, take responsibility for them, and change it! This is the way to get what you want! The moment you take total and complete responsibility for every result in every area of your life is the moment you begin to get what you want.

We must take control of everything we can control and then let go of everything else. If we can't control it, then we can still control how we choose to respond to it. When it comes to other people, for example, what others do, say, or think, is their responsibility, not ours. We have no control over that. Have you heard the comment, "Life would be great if it weren't for other people?" Well, I wonder how that is working out? Do people still make you really mad? Do others really have that much control over your emotional state? Do they really have that much power over you? We have the power to control our attitude, our mood, and every emotion we feel.

The next time you get ready to react to what someone else did, remind yourself that you are being tested on self-control and this person is your teacher. Pass the test! Become a master of Jedi mind control, and play the game of responding to someone proactively. Don't react to them. Take their communication in, assess their words and emotions and ask yourself what they need. Respond knowing your response will be the cure to what they need. For example, someone begins to yell at you. They are really saying, "I'm scared, hurt, and feeling out of control."

Instead of yelling back, your response is one that addresses these emotions. Your response is one that will get the outcome you want. Your response is one to get this person back to sanity.

This realization that you are in control is a game changer. Do you plan your days or just let them happen? Instead of saying, "Have a nice day," start saying, "Make it a great day!" We are the captains of our ship. We control the direction of our ship by the choices we make. We do create our destiny. Will the next five choices you make help or hurt the life you want to create? Each choice we make throughout our lives has a consequence, whether it is positive or negative. Control your choices. Every choice we make in life starts a motion that will come back to us in some way. Are you living your life today to create the life you want tomorrow? We really do create the quality of our life by the choices we make every day. If you like or don't like your life, what choices are you making that are contributing to that? For example, you could respond back in a soft voice with, "This situation is upsetting. How can I make this better?

RESPONSIBILITY

When we break down the word responsibility, it means our *ability* to *respond*. For some, the word responsibility brings on dread and obligation. It doesn't work to think of it that way. Responsibility is literally your ability to respond. Someone who practices high responsibility has very strong relationships in their life. They have good results in all areas of their life. They recognize their states or moods and deliberately choose to stay in that state or change it. They have mastered their ability to respond. They have become proactive versus reactive. They are constantly monitoring their states and making sure their responses are getting them closer to what they want. This level of thought is transformational. This level of thought will keep you from yelling at your loved ones or trying to win an argument with your spouse, for example. By the way, you can never *win* an argument with your spouse. You will always loose if you are "*winning*" against your spouse. Just keeping it real, folks.

Whenever we experience an event, the event does not determine our response. Our *interpretation of the event* determines our response. This is humongo! Our brains are wired to receive an outside stimulus, interpret the event, and then experience the emotion of what our interpretation is to that event. Very few of us have mastered this level of responsibility. This takes lifetime mastery. Most of us receive an outside stimulus and then react to it emotionally without even realizing why we are responding that way. Masters of breaking this stimulus/response cycle have learned to recognize the stimulus as it comes in, and then have learned to consciously respond to it.

For example, if someone frowns at you, do you get upset and frown back? This is an example of bypassing the interpretation of the stimulus. The next time someone frowns at you, recognize that you were just frowned at; recognize that it is up to you to interpret that event, and then choose your response. Can you interpret the other person's frown as someone who is having a bad day? Maybe they are constipated. Maybe they were dropped on their head as a baby. Who knows? Your response is based on how you interpret the event.

If you constantly see events as personal attacks against you, then you are not going to be very happy. If someone cuts you off in traffic, do you really think that the other driver thought to themselves, "Ha, ha, I'm going to totally cut this person off and put us both in danger!" Does that interpretation of the event work? I think you get the idea. Once we change the way we view the world, the world we view changes. Once we recognize that we don't see the world as the world is, we see the world as we are; we put ourselves back in control.

STEPS TO BREAKING THE NEGATIVE STIMULUS/ RESPONSE CYCLE:

1. Recognize that an event has just stimulated your brain.

2. Recognize your immediate negative emotion.

3. Mentally interpret the event in a way that gives you a positive emotion.

4. Choose your response.

CONQUERING STRESS

Once we begin to practice consciously receiving a stimulus, interpreting the event in a way that works for us, and then choosing our response, we can take it a step further and learn to recognize some of our non-serving coping mechanisms that are giving us our *current* results. For example, the next time you begin to feel resistance or stress, acknowledge it instead of jumping right to some of the popular coping mechanisms like: disbelief, denial, anger, avoidance, self-righteousness, rationalization, projection on others, or worry. When you're pressed, do any of these reactions below sound familiar to you?

AUTOMATIC REACTING COPING MECHANISMS

1. Disbelief —"No way. I don't believe it."

2. Denial—"This is not really happening to me even though I see what is going on."

3. Anger—"Why is everyone all over me? I am furious!"

4. Avoidance—"Let's just forget about this. I don't want to talk about it."

5. Self-righteousness—"Everyone is stupid. The masses are asses. No one knows what the hell they are talking about. They don't have a clue!"

6. Rationalization—"Well, it really isn't that bad. I am only doing this because I need to right now."

7. Projection on others—"Look, this isn't really about me, it's about you. Why are *you* so stressed?"

8. Worry—"I just can't sleep at night. I don't know what is going to happen."

Once we feel the emotion of resistance or stress, find out why. What is causing that emotion? Doesn't this make more sense than going right to the non-serving coping mechanisms? Once we find out what is causing the resistance or stress, we can work toward fixing it. In most cases, stress is fear. Fear is uncertainty. And uncertainty is lack of planning on your part.

So much of getting what we want is just being totally accepting of ourselves and understanding that no one has it all figured out. We are all works in progress. We are all on the same planet, getting challenged by the same things in different ways. This is pretty spectacular when you *really, finally, totally, undoubtedly* accept this about yourself and everyone around you.

When the preparation is done, the test is easy. When you are certain that everything will turn out the way it is *supposed* to, then you are at peace. Once you accept worst-case scenario,

> *Control what you can, and trust that whatever you can't control will turn out for the best.*

then no more worries. Expect the best, but prepare for the worst, remember? Another way to say it is to expect the best and accept the worst-case scenario.

Why worry about something that is out of your control? Your worrying is not going to change the outcome. Why worry about something that is in your control? Your worrying is not going to change the outcome. If you feel stressed or negative resistance then analyze it. Control what you can, and trust that whatever you can't control will turn out for the best.

If you are dealing with automatic-reacting coping mechanisms, recognize what is causing the negative charge in your mind. Accept the situation, forgive yourself and others, take responsibility, and create a new action. I know this sounds too easy, and it really isn't that easy. It is simple, but not easy. The key is to recognize it and then ask yourself if you want to keep living that way. If you do, than no one is going to be able to help you. If you are ready to change and go after what you want, then get some support. Follow the steps. *Elevate* your life.

I just realized I have invented a disease called, Automatic Reacting Coping Mechanisms Disorder, or ARCMD. When the drug companies develop a drug for this diagnosis, you will now know how to handle it the natural way, with no side effects.

CHANGE THE STORY

Have you ever been in a bad mood and don't know why? The next time you are in a bad mood, recognize that the mood is not serving you. Ask yourself what stimulus just triggered that thought and emotion. Every experience we have shapes our perception of reality. Following every experience, we set ourselves up to have the same perception for all other similar experiences. If those original experiences were perceived as negative then change your story about the past event that is playing in your mind.

For some of us, we have so many perceived bad experiences that we are always in a bad mood as a result of so many subconscious stimuli. For example, maybe your girlfriend or boyfriend broke up with you abruptly in a blue Volkswagen. You remember the event and you remember the blue Volkswagen. You remember how crushed you felt and how you were depressed for months. You have since moved on but never completely resolved the event in your mind. When you think about the old flame, you still have a negative charge associated with the thought. Now, subconsciously, every time you see a blue Volkswagen, you are sad and you don't know why because you haven't connected the dots. Change the story.

These unconscious memories can work for happiness as well. Do you have a familiar song that comes on the radio and all of a sudden you are in a state of joy? You are happy because that song was played during really fun times for you in your past. Your emotions of happiness that you experienced when you first heard that song are still linked to that particular song today.

Really monitor your emotions, especially if you are not sure why you are feeling sad. Begin to make the connections of what just made your state change to sadness or anger. The more you dig at this, the more answers and "aha" moments will come your way. As soon as you recognize what current stimulus is attached to the old negative event, you can change your story about it, confront it, forgive it, and move on.

When people sometimes have so many negative memories everywhere they look, it is beneficial for them to put themselves in a different environment after they have addressed the original experience in their mind. Try the beach instead of the mountains, for example. This isn't running if you have confronted all of the experiences. This is a new start, if you will.

I recently had an experience with an old associate and mentor of mine. Basically, my associate went to work for my original mentor, all without me knowing about it. I was given no notice and really thought I knew them both better than I obviously did. I initially felt betrayed and angry about the whole experience that had happened. A few days after this event happened, I confronted them both at their office. I said what I had to say, listened, and then squashed it in my mind. The next day, I was able to forgive them both as well as myself, and I truly wished them both the best. The event actually served me really well.

I thought I had dealt with it completely and was ready to move on. On my route to work, I drove past their office every day. Each time I passed the intersection, I would get resistance, stress, and a negative charge. I wasn't sure why and then I realized that I was still upset about this.

Subconsciously, I was getting upset every time I drove past this intersection. It was a pretty awesome moment to realize. I realized that although I had forgiven them and myself, I still felt like I had been betrayed. My perception of the event was that I was betrayed. That story was keeping me in a negative state each time I passed that intersection. It was time to change my story. Instead of thinking that I was betrayed, I instead thought of how I had the strength and courage to confront them both and stand up for myself. This new story now empowered me and made me feel good about myself. Now every time I pass that intersection, I feel great. Seriously, this was magical to me. Do you have any stories you need to change?

LAW OF ATTRACTION

I am going to close this chapter with the law of attraction. I'm sure you've heard about it by now. I am including it in this chapter because it is a choice that we consciously or unconsciously make every day. What you think about, you attract into your life. It has widely been taught as a spiritual principal and it has been shown scientifically as well. It is a law just like the law of gravity. You can't see it but it exists. Our brain becomes wired to search for what we focus on. Our brain waves literally have vibrations that can be measured. Thoughts that make you feel good have different vibrations than thoughts that make you feel bad. Both vibrations attract the same quality of vibrations. Positive people do not like to be around negative people, for example. Major negative thoughts literally repulse people who are experiencing major positive thoughts. As an aside, the next time you are around some really negative vibrations, don't run from the person; instead, give them the opportunity to *Elevate*! You could say, "Hmm, that is interesting. Have you thought about it like this?" If they continue with major negativity, then at least you know you have planted a seed. I remember one time I was being particularly negative and really defending my position, really wanting to be right. The person I was talking to said. "Okay, I give up, but let me ask you, is this way of thinking working for you?" My lesson was received.

Whatever we focus on, we tend to get more of. When you focus on what you want, your mind will become alert to the many opportunities that will come your way as a result of this focus. Some say that the opportunities were always there, and now once you focus on them, you are more aware of them. And some say that when you ignite this law of attraction and focus on what you want, the power of God steps in and lines up opportunities for you to take action on. Sounds a lot like prayer, doesn't it? The choice is yours. It works. Focus on what you want. What does not work is for you to sit in a corner and focus on what you want and not get off of your butt to make it happen and take advantage of the incoming opportunities!

Your most dominate thoughts will definitely move your life in that direction. If you think about success and how you are going to achieve it, you will have opportunities in that area come your way. If you think that people are rude, you will see rudeness everywhere you see people. If you think people have an abundance of love in them, you will see unconditional love everywhere you see people.

The law of attraction works. Whether viewing it spiritually or scientifically, you have the ability to achieve what you want. You have the ability to constantly focus on what you want. You have the ability to take action on the opportunities that will arise from focusing on what you want. Deliberately, intentionally, focus on what you want.

> **Bottom line:** You have been given the ability to recognize why you think the way you do. You have been given the ability to be in control of your choices and to choose your response. Guard and protect your thoughts and think like a winner.

11 Chapter Eleven:
Attitude and Happiness

"Today is the beginning of a new day. God has given me this day to use as I see fit. I can waste it or grow in its light and be of service to others. Today is important because I am exchanging a day of my life for it. When tomorrow comes, today will be gone forever. I hope I don't regret the price I paid for it."

—6th Grade Outdoor Education Camp Leader

–Jefferson County, 1986

Every morning for over twenty-five years now, I've been saying the above quote. Okay, not *every* morning. It was given to me along with the rest of my sixth grade class on a little piece of laminated paper during outdoor education week. I love that we have no idea how and when a little note of encouragement can grow in someone's life and affect so many others. The morning affirmation above shaped my attitude from a very young age. Attitude really is everything, isn't it? As we work our way through these chapters, your current attitude now will be a reflection of how much you are absorbing from the previous chapters. So far we have explored some possible areas in our life that could use some improvement. Attitude is our reflection of those improvements. Coming soon will be the awesome results from our continuation of practicing a great attitude. People with great attitudes get what they want.

So how is your attitude most of the time? As you know, we all have thoughts. Our outward expressions of our thoughts show us our attitude. So if we have to think, which most of us do, then we might as well think good thoughts and practice a good attitude. They really are contagious. A great attitude starts with recognizing that every day is truly a gift. Every day truly is a new day. It is up to us to seize, grasp, and enjoy every moment of it. Clap your hands and say, "Yes! Yes! Yes!" Really, do it. I'll wait. Okay, feels awesome doesn't it? Attitude is about positive expectation. It is about gratefulness. It is about doing the things that make us happy. It's time for success! Did you know that seventy-five percent of your success rate is based on your belief in yourself, your associations, and your attitude? Twenty-five percent of your success is based on your IQ.[9] Sounds like we better pay attention if we want to get what we want.

MORNING ATTITUDE

Do you wake up every morning to an alarm clock or an opportunity clock? Do you wake up knowing you can accomplish any goal you set? Do you expect to be blessed so you can be a blessing? If not, start tomorrow morning. No, start now! Say to yourself, "I CAN accomplish any goal I set! I DO expect to be blessed today!" It's all about attitude. For some of you, this may be over the top. If it is, be patient, you'll get there if you choose. All great things develop over time with consistency.

> *Say to yourself, "I CAN accomplish any goal I set! I DO expect to be blessed today!"*

It is important to start our attitude off in the morning because a single thought in the morning can make or break our entire day! If we start the morning off with a bad memory, for example, and replay the memory in our head all day, we'll continue to expect what we are already getting. Change it. Your attitude can be optimistic or pessimistic. It is totally your choice. How you feel most of the time is a direct result of your attitude. Optimistic people scientifically are happier, healthier, and wealthier. They have stronger energy, are enthusiastic, and have stronger immune systems. I would like to choose this one, please.

One morning recently I came into work a little overwhelmed. *Who, you?* Yes, totally. I work downtown in an office that was built in the 1950s. It was Denver's first skyscraper. Of course it has gone through some remodeling; however, they have kept a little bit of its nostalgia, especially in the inside of the elevators. As I was riding up the refurbished elevator, I couldn't help but think of the men in their hats and the women in their dresses all shuffling into work on a similar morning fifty years ago. I'm sure most of the people who worked in my building in the 1950s are long gone now, just memories to all they touched. It reminded me to enjoy the process. It reminded me that I am not the first, nor certainly the last, to feel a little overwhelmed at times.

My attitude turned quickly to that of joy. I remembered to seize the day! I remembered that we will all be food for worms. I remembered that this will be the last morning on this particular date that I will ever have. I remembered that today *is* the beginning of a new day!

HAPPY HAPPY JOY JOY

Do you know what makes you happy? Have you ever listed out the specific people, places, and things that you enjoy? Do you schedule those into your life? If we are feeling that we *need* a vacation for example, we are already behind. Schedule your vacations or vacation days now. If you have the liberty to schedule them for a year out, this will always put you in the driver's seat, avoiding burn out. So many of us, including myself, seem to race through life, but we don't want to get to the end. So many of us race to the finish line not realizing the finish line is death! Schedule a little weekend off every three months at a minimum, if you can. We all really do have our own unique ways of making ourselves happy. This prescheduling your vacations is like hitting the reset button.

Did you know that we also have universal principles that make us happy when practiced? Do you want to know how to be happy most of the time? Of course you do! Let's get started. First of all, being happy does not mean you walk around ecstatic all day long. Happiness is a balance. It is not total elevation during all waking hours. This is important to clarify.

THE BASICS

If you want lifelong happiness, my suggestion is to completely absorb the *Elevate* lifestyle and live what you have learned so far in this book. These are the qualities that will bring inner joy. True happiness starts with what happens inside of you, not outside of you. The principles of Parts One and Two will give internal joy: Practicing Love, Practicing Character, Following Your Moral Code; Forgiving Yourself and Forgiving Others; Totally Accepting Yourself and Not Seeking Approval From Others; Believing in Yourself; Knowing Your Gifts and Exercising Them; Developing a Strong Faith; and Knowing Your Purpose. These principles are the keys that unlock everything else. These are also the principles that can take a lifetime to master. No one is asking you to be a master. I am asking you to dive in and get started, though. Remember, you're worth it! These are the basics.

SMILE

It feels good to smile. It increases your face value big time! Your brain has what science calls mirror neurons. When someone smiles at us, it makes our brain think that it is smiling and makes us feel happy. When we smile at others it makes *us* feel happy *and* the person we are smiling at feel happy. You know what is really cool? When someone observes us smiling at someone *else*; it makes *them* feel happy too! Holy cow, the next time you are on the jumbo-tron at your local sporting event, smile! You will affect tens of thousands!

PRACTICE GRATEFULNESS

A key to happiness is being totally grateful for who you are and what you have now. This doesn't mean that you cannot become or desire more, it just means that you are totally grateful for who you are and what you have now. If you are an American, for example, you can be grateful that you have freedom, you speak English, you understand currency, and you live in a country where you can achieve your dreams. What are you grateful for? Are you grateful for your health, your family, your career, and/or your relationship with God? What overwhelms *you* with gratefulness? Gratefulness is the fastest way I know of to get back to the state of happiness.

NOW AND FUTURE

Decide to be happy now. Successful people are happy before they are "successful." Happy people are happy now AND they are future driven. If we become a spectator of life, we just need to get back to the game. Jump back in and get clear on the direction you are headed. Positive expectation is a huge part of happiness. What are you looking forward to?

QUALITY OF LIFE

Take some time and figure out what quality of life makes you happy. The quality of your life is a direct reflection of the things, experiences, and the environment you create. These things must deliberately happen. Create the moments and memories that you will never forget. When you are interested in something, pursue it! The things you are happy with, you are interested in. The things you are typically not happy with, you are not interested in.

PRODUCTION

A key to happiness is productivity. When you add value to your work, church, or organization, you are happy. When you are producing something that you are proud of, you are happy. This is why actively achieving your goals is so important. Happiness is moving toward what you want.

HELP OTHERS

It makes you happy to help others. If there are any areas of your life that you are not happy in, find someone to help in this area. You will be helping them, you will be helping yourself, and you will be experiencing happiness.

BREAK THE FUNK

This one is great. If you ever feel like you are in a funk and happiness is escaping you, here is how you can get happy again, today! Do one of the following: meet someone new that is interesting and funny; do an experience you have not done before; buy a new outfit; and/or do something you are afraid to do. If you take action and do one of these things when you feel like you are in a funk, you will snap out of it right away. It sounds simple. It is! Do it!

Happiness does not come naturally to many of us. Happiness does take effort. These few things above have certainly been my formula. Anyone who knows me knows me to be a pretty happy person. I smile all the time. Seriously. It disturbs some people that I smile so much. I have been asked many times by people I am just getting to know, what makes me so happy. Well, everything you just read is it. Happiness really does have a formula. Choose to be happy. Begin today to start to do the things that make you happy.

HIGH SCHOOL HAPPY

I was talking to a friend recently who wasn't too happy about his life anymore. We did get to the bottom of it. It is pretty straight forward if you follow the items above. I said before that this book is a movement. The *Elevate* life is a movement. Follow the principles, and happiness is yours. While I was talking to my friend about getting back to happiness, he kept saying how happy he was in high school. So we found out why.

I have to admit, high school was awesome. You either loved it or hated it, right? For those of us who loved it, have you asked yourself why?

There are many reasons why high school was a happy time for many of us. The key is making the effort to now duplicate what made us happy in high school. For example, high school comes with a lot of variety and first experiences. We were spoon fed different classes to learn from, dances to attend, extra-curricular activities like sports, drama, debate, choir, band, etc. High school is very social and very productive. High school comes with much fear to overcome yet also numerous dreams to accomplish and community outreach programs to participate in. High school met our needs as a human being to experience: certainty, variety, connection, significance, growth, and contribution.

The key to getting back to high school happy is recreating all of that on a regular basis. I know we have more barriers now than we had in high school but not enough to make it an excuse. Experience new things again. When was the last time you did something for the first time? Join local sports clubs or organizations, or local theaters, choirs, or bands. Step up to fear again. Get clear on what you want again and go after it. Volunteer again, produce, accomplish. Your happiness is your responsibility. Go get it!

As an aside, I heard a radio commercial the other day talking about taking a supplement to get back to high school skinny. I hope you know that for most of us that is a myth. Have you looked at a high school kid lately? They still look like kids. They haven't stopped growing yet. For some of us, if we were the same weight we were in high school, we would look emaciated! If you are unhappy because of your weight, then get after it. I'll show you how to stay motivated on that one later.

BARRIERS

Throughout this book we have talked about some of the barriers to happiness. Once we recognize what is keeping us from being happy, we can fix it, right? Right! Begin with what you are not doing in this chapter if you want to be happy. In addition to that, let's look at a few quicksand pits that when not recognized can take us off track.

PERFECTIONISM

I like to perform the secondary interviews at our company, Discover Health and Wellness. As I get to know the candidates, many say they are a perfectionist and think that is a good thing. It seems to be a buzzword of some sort. Let me fill you in on a little clue. That is not a good thing! If you consider yourself a perfectionist, consider it one of your areas of improvement that needs to be tweaked. There is no such thing as perfect. You will never be perfect. Even if you think you performed to perfection, there is always a next level. Your self-worth does not come from your performance. You do not need to seek approval from others. Stop following the myth.

Perfectionism is a huge source of unhappiness. It can also be called having a fear of failure. It generally starts with wanting something, and then being afraid to fail at it, and then procrastinating on it, and then beating yourself up with criticism because you are not taking action, and then feeling anxious and bummed out, and then feeling loss of self-esteem, and then more procrastination or even avoidance, and then ultimately unhappiness.

If you battle with this, know that you are a work in progress. Every time you fail, you can fold or you can learn from your mistakes. Learn how to do it better next time. Know that your self-worth comes from loving God, yourself, and others, not your performance. Seek your own approval by doing your best and forgetting the rest. Please don't take this lightly. Perfectionism is not healthy. I admire the fact that perfectionists want to do their best, but this pattern leads to guaranteed unhappiness. The only thing any of us are perfect at is being a human being.

Many producers and high performers share this trait. It's a simple fix but not easy. It just needs to be accepted and then it can be tweaked. Every leader in the history books failed more than they succeeded. This is how we learn. Every time you "fail" you figure out a way to not do it next time. Would you ever tell a baby to stop attempting to walk because the little bubba keeps falling? If you do have kids, help to break this cycle by beginning to ask them if they did their best, instead of whether they won or lost. I'll discuss more about raising kids the *Elevate* way later.

> *Every time you "fail" you figure out a way to not do it next time.*

SEEKING TOO MUCH CONTROL

Okay, control freaks, let's knock this one out of the park. Stop! Stop! Stop trying to control everything in your life! Control is important and whatever you can't control, controls you; however, that is okay! The need to control everything is usually because there are areas of our life that are out of control. Seriously. Of course you want to control things in your life. We all want to create certainty where we can. However, accept the parts of your life that are beyond your control. Our happiness not only comes from our level of certainty of control in our life, but our level of us being certain that we cannot control everything. We can still have certainty knowing that we are certain that this situation is one that we cannot control. So number one, be happy and know that what you cannot control, roll with. Get on a Mach 6 rollercoaster for a while and say good-bye to control. Have you ever wondered why most control freaks don't like rollercoasters? They can't control them!

So what area of your life are you totally out of control in? For example, is your lack of discipline in your health and fitness life leading you to over discipline your kids? Is your lack of control over your finances leading you to be an overbearing controller with your coworkers? Address the areas in your life that you self-admittedly know you are not doing too well in. Accept the fact that you are a work in progress, and if you choose to, you are getting better and better. Once you accept this about the certain area of your life that is not going so hot, you will not have the need to control everyone else around you. Bam!

LACK OF CONFRONTATION

Fear of confrontation is a huge trap for so many of us. I have seen this one totally destroy relationships. Your happiness with others is directly proportionate to your ability to confront when needed. Confrontation must happen to get what you want. Instead of looking at it as a scary negative thing, let's take the mystery out of it and make it a not scary, positive thing. Lack of confrontation leads to gossip and all sorts of damage. If you need to deal with someone that is causing you stress, you have got to do it. It can be a huge barrier to happiness.

For the love of God, please tackle this pillar of self-growth. Not confronting someone leads directly to unhappiness. We must be willing, as humans, to experience anything. There is a huge growth opportunity for you in confronting your lack of confrontation with others. Lovingly confront others if you need to. Tell them what your experience was with them and how you feel about it. Never question their intention and ask where they were coming from. The moment we confront something, it is over. All the pain and agony we carry around from not confronting someone on a disagreement or challenge is literally gone the moment we confront them.

Remember, you tell people how you allow yourself to be treated. For example, there are some people you know you could be late to the appointment for and others you know you better never be late for, correct? Your ability to confront lets people know that you respect them and expect them to respect you. It lets them know you value them and expect them to value you. If you are constantly needing to confront someone then they either don't know what your rules are because you haven't told them, or you are just not that important to them. Good friends can make you happy. The slight moment of being uncomfortable is well worth the long lasting gain of their relationship.

If you are feeling a negative charge toward someone, and you care about them, don't they deserve to know about it? Confrontation is about loving someone enough to get on the same page with them. Non-confrontation leads to destruction. Consider not confronting someone an early death of the relationship. If someone has done something that caused a negative charge in you, consider it the seed of a nasty weed that, if not pulled out, will grow into sarcasm, negativity, criticalness, and gossip about the other person. If you have fallen into this trap, the only people that put up with others that are regularly sarcastic, negative, critical and like to gossip, do it themselves regularly! So now you have created a life of relationships that attract this mode of thought only because you are not pulling out the weeds when it is time to confront.

These types of people that are stuck in this negative pattern do not get what they want and are not happy. Help them by being the example of someone who cares enough about themselves and others to confront, lovingly. Not confronting not only destroys the relationship with the person you are not confronting, but destroys your future by the type of person it makes you and by the type of people it attracts. This is hardcore, but true, folks. I care enough about you to tell you the truth. The most successful people in the world know how to confront. They see lack of confrontation as the deadly trap that it is.

Step up and know that you need to care enough about those closest to you to be able to tell them how you feel. Being passive aggressive always leads to drama and usually leads to explosion. The following is a formula to lovingly confront anyone in your life. It has been instrumental for me. When you get a negative charge, recognize it and don't let it get to your emotional state. Deal with it head-on without emotion and never question their intent. Remember, what you don't confront, controls you. Some things are no big deal and you need to be the one to decide when you want to confront or not. My trigger is when I begin to get a negative charge around them or the same thing is happening consistently. That is when I know that if I value them, I owe it to both of us to bring it up.

Follow the following script formula and watch the angst dissolve and the friendship strengthen.

1. Let them know you value them.

2. Bring up what your experience was with them and how you felt about it.

3. Find out where they were coming from.

4. Get back into a mutual agreement, moving forward.

Example: "Hey, Sally, I think you are a great friend and I value the time we spend together. Something happened the other day that I wanted to touch base with you about. The other day when you cut me off during conversation and never called me back made me feel a little upset and disrespected. I value our friendship and I would never question your intention. I just wanted to see where you were coming from. Okay, I figured so. No worries. When that happened, it really threw me off my game. So anyway, moving forward, can we agree to not cut each other off and if we do make sure we both call each other afterwards? Great, let's go to the beach now."

Example: "Hey, Joe. You know how great of friends we are, right? Okay, yesterday, when you cancelled on me last minute again, it made me a little upset. I know it was not intentional; however, where were you coming from? Okay, that's what I thought. Moving forward, can we agree to not cancel on each other last minute? Great, let's go have a beer."

LACK OF INTEGRITY:

I spent quite a bit of time on this one in the Character chapter. Here's a quick summary. If what you say, think, and do is not consistent, you will not be happy. Contradiction in your life equals self-destruction if not addressed. You must be right with yourself to be happy. If you do battle with this, it is called being a human being. The degree to how far it is off will determine your level of unhappiness. If this is one area you still need to work on, check out the Happiness Through Character section in Chapter Two.

> **Bottom line:** Attitude begins with our choice to have a good one. Happiness begins with taking action to deliberately make ourselves happy. There are barriers to happiness that may be keeping you from experiencing what you want. Handle them and carry on, my friend.

Chapter Twelve:
Creating Congruent Programs

"Indecision may or may not be my problem."
-Jimmy Buffett

I have been excited to write this chapter for quite some time now. Over the years, I have wrestled with several conflicting programs. Some things that were taught to me have worked really well and some have not. I hope some of the distinctions that I have made create clarity for you as they have done for me. As you already know, we have the choice on how we want to think. How you think gives you the results in your life.

> *A good rule to follow is to think like someone who has what you want in that area of their life.*

A good rule to follow is to think like someone who has what you want in that area of their life. If someone has a great spiritual life and it is evident by the results in their life, ask them their thoughts on spirituality. If someone is super fit and you can literally grate cheese off their abs, ask them how they think about health and fitness. If someone has gobs of cash, ask them their thoughts on moolah. If someone is voted the best husband and daddy in the world, ask them how they think about family.

We all have a fundamental premise on what we believe for every category of our life. If we have not created certainty about what programs run our mind for the important areas of our life, it is happening without you knowing it. Have you heard, "When it rains, it pours!" or "All bad things come in threes!" or "Things have been going really well, I'm waiting for something bad to happen now." When you are going through a challenge in life, do you really want to think that it is going to start pouring on you now? Or do you really want to think that after every challenge you're going to get two more challenges back-to-back? Do you really want to think that when things are going well, a challenge is around the corner? Of course not! We all have hundreds of these little thought programs that we live by. Our job is to make sure we are conscious of them and that they are serving us.

We're going to explore a few areas of life and get certain about what we believe about them. We are going to get certain about how we think about each area. If we don't like how we are currently thinking in each area, hit the delete button and reboot. The best way to see how you think in each category of life is to ask yourself if you like the results you are getting in that area. We touched on this in the Choice and Responsibility chapter. When we are certain about where we stand and how we think, we are in control. When we are in control, we get what we want.

THE FUNDAMENTAL PROGRAMS

The following are my programs for the top four areas of my life that I focus on the most. This is how I think in these categories. These programs have served me well. I share them as an example. What are your programs for these areas? After reading these, either hit the download button or start programming your own. As soon as you are certain about the program, remember, your thoughts become your feelings, your feelings become your actions and actions become your results! Thoughts really do become things. Choose the good thoughts!

GOD

1. God represents: Unconditional Love, Strength, Wisdom, Encouragement, Security, Guidance, Peace, and Understanding.
2. God's number one and two commandments are to love Him and treat others how you want to be treated.
3. My faith in action, by helping my fellow man and utilizing my gifts and talents, is more important to God than what name I call Him or spiritual practice I follow.

HEALTH

1. When I am strong and vibrant physically, I am strong and vibrant in every area of my life.
2. It is my responsibility to take excellent care of the body I was given for myself, my family, and all those I love.

3. My health is elevated by: avoiding toxins, maintaining my spine and nervous system through chiropractic adjustments, eating lean, clean and green, exercising regularly, and living the *Elevate* mindset.

FAMILY

1. Extraordinary relationships require extraordinary peoplc.
2. Family is a gift for the purpose of life-long happiness and growth together.
3. Family is based on: unconditional love and commitment, communication, and total acceptance of one another with a shared purpose and vision.

WEALTH

1. Money is a tool of exchange for goods and services sold, and by itself, has nothing to do with good or bad.
2. Money · represents: achievement, production, the entrepreneurial spirit, freedom, and America.
3. My relationship with money is a healthy, loving one and money flows to me because I manage it well.

MORE PROGRAMS

Let's take a look as some subtle incongruent programs that may not be very well defined for us. These are the day-to-day thoughts we have on a variety of topics. Enjoy!

LIVE TODAY LIKE IT IS YOUR LAST

Have you heard to live today like it was the last day of your life? Well, this is actually true. What date is it? Well, whatever date you are reading this is absolutely the last day you will ever live this date for the rest of your life. As I write, I am living the last July 14, 2013 I will ever live for the rest of my life! Unless we create a time machine, this is our current truth. Live today like it is your last is meant to inspire us to not hold back, to go for it, to seize the day! Where it gets confusing is when it is taken too literally. Do you know anyone who has taken this quote a bit too literally and lives their life like this? It has been my experience that they are a lot of fun but don't have much direction.

I love the idea of living only for today and following your heart, but when the head and the heart don't line up, we need to examine why. The whole philosophy of just do what feels right, does not work if it is not balanced out with intellect. When it feels right but your head is saying no, then don't do it. When it feels right and your head is uncertain, give it a little thought and then decide if you want to go for it or not. When it feels right and your head is certain, do it and do it now!

I'm sure many of us have heard the motivational question, "If you had six months to live, what would you do?" Great question! The key is to plan the things out that you would do and truly do live them now! If you have known someone with a diagnosis of cancer, for example, and they have been given six months to live, you know that those last six months are not very fulfilling. If you have been uncertain about anything, it is time to get certain and decide on what direction you are going to take now. Today really could by your last.

When my Dad died, he was almost seventy-five-years old. I was prepared for years to receive the news of his passing just based on his age and lifestyle alone. I said everything I needed to say and so did he *years ago*. We created time together and took fabulous life dream trips *years ago*. My relationship with him was one that I really did live each day like it was our last.

If you died today, are you leaving anything unsaid? If you died today, would you be totally satisfied that you went for it? If you died today, would you say you lived a life worth living? Dive deep!

Live your greatest life with full expression like it was your last, but plan like you had one hundred more years to enjoy it!

COMPETITIVE VERSUS NON-COMPETITIVE

My boys love soccer. We are now at the age where some of the kids, and parents, are much more competitive than others are. Have you ever heard a six-year-old soccer player yell, "Let's kill them this game!" Any thoughts on that? Yeah, let's explore this one a little. Healthy competition is a good thing, and unhealthy competition, not so much. Did you know that the original meaning of the word compete means, "to strive together." That definition changes the way we think about competition, doesn't it? Competition doesn't have to be about vengeance and anger.

Let's take soccer for example. It is good to be motivated to win the game; just make sure you do your best. If you do your best, you did win the game. You won *your* game regardless of the end score. Do your kids a favor, don't ask them if they won, ask them if they did their best, right? When we go up against competitors that have the same or better skill set than we do, we usually perform better and have a great time doing it. Healthy competition means that you want to not only do as good as your opponent, but you want to do better! This kind of competition takes us to the next level. This kind of competition pushes greatness as you "strive together."

Some competitors align with the concept of not competing at all and just go out to have fun. Well, this is fine, but these are the kids that end up sitting on the bench. Trust me; I was one of them. I'm afraid I was a bench warmer in most sports I played until I found martial arts. It is much better to compete knowing you are going to give it your all, instead of not giving it your all because you are just out there to have fun. There are times to do both and those times are when everyone on the team is in agreement. For example, while playing volleyball at the family reunion, don't slam the ball into your grandma's head and scream, "In your face!"

SELFISH VERSUS SELF-INTEREST

This one can plague you. Are you in it to win it at all costs, or are you a team player? Do you serve everyone else but yourself because you don't want to be selfish, or do you take care of yourself first? Do you take the last piece of pizza or leave it for someone else that is hungry?

Here's my take on it. Being selfish versus having a strong self-interest comes down to moral code, character and manners. A strong self-interest means that you love yourself enough to take care of yourself *before* anyone else, so that you *can* take care of everyone else. Put your oxygen mask on first, right? Selfish means you have no regard for others. This is quite different from having a strong self-interest. If you are going after what you want but sacrificing your character by hurting others in the process, then stop. *Elevate* and recognize that you have slipped into selfishness. One cure for selfishness is to get out of scarcity thinking and practice abundance. There is more than enough for everyone, regardless of what reality TV is teaching us.

If you are going after what you want but sacrificing your character by hurting others in the process, then stop.

Have you heard that there is no such thing as a selfless act? Well, this is true. This isn't a bad thing; it is reality. Everything we do is to make ourselves feel good. Life really is all about you. The key is to not confuse this reality as being selfish. Recognize it as having a strong self-interest, which is good. But wait a minute, you say, "I help people. How can that be about me?" Don't get me wrong, this entire book is about getting successful yourself so you can help people, but don't pretend that as you help people, it doesn't make *you* feel good in the process.

Here's the final distinction between being selfish and having a strong self-interest. You have got to take care of yourself first *and* be considerate to others *without* being sacrificial to yourself. Practice abundance and know that there is more than enough! The difference between self-interest and selfishness is, self-interest is taking care of yourself while being considerate towards others and selfishness is taking care of yourself with no consideration towards others.

USE YOUR BEST JUDGMENT VERSUS DON'T JUDGE OTHERS

The definition of judgment means to form an opinion or estimation after careful consideration. I would like to add, "after careful consideration *and* observation." Using your best judgment is vital for success. It is right. It becomes wrong when we judge someone's *intent* based on financial status, race, sexual preference, or gender. This is called judging someone based on a stereotype. This type of judgment in these categories will end poorly for you. For example, if you had a bad experience with a financially rich Caucasian lesbian, that does not mean that you will have a bad experience with all financially rich Caucasian lesbians.

So is it okay to judge others if I am using my best judgment? Yes! To get what we want we *need to* use our best judgment. I judge others based on the results in their life. I do it, you do it, and everyone you meet is doing it to you. Use your best judgment with others based on the choices they are making in their life. This is called forming an opinion after careful consideration and observation.

For example, I recently have gotten to know one of my neighbors better. He has consistently done what he said he was going to do. He is committed to his family with all of his heart and it is evident by observing his relationship with his wife and daughters. Based on my estimation and observation, I have judged him to be a stand-up strong character man. On the other hand, let's say, you meet someone who does not honor their commitments, doesn't show up on time, exaggerates everything, and doesn't bathe regularly. I think it would be safe to say that using your best judgment, you could surmise that this person has a fair amount of work to do on their life.

Where we get into trouble is when we become self-righteous about judging others, thinking that we are better than they are based on the results in their life. This is flat out wrong. Remember, we are all works in progress, and you may be better at some things where they are better at other things. Usually, we use our best judgment toward others to see if they are someone we want to be around or want to be like. Like attracts like.

Appearance, whether we like it or not, is probably the most judged trait there is. Knowing this, we need to make it work for us so we can get what we want. Appearance equals persuasion. If you walk like a duck and talk like a duck, then you are probably a duck. We need to be very cautious of how we choose to represent ourselves to the world. People treat us based on how we portray ourselves.

As I said before, I believe it is wrong to stereotype people based on financial status, race, sexual preference, and gender. I do believe in most cases, though, it is pretty accurate to stereotype people based on how they *want to portray themselves* in appearance to others. For example, most thugs look like thugs. Do you want to dress like a thug if you are not a thug? Why would you want to appear like a thug if you were not a thug?

Our appearance shapes our personality, hands down. My sister loves to ride Harleys. She will be the first one to admit that when she has all of her leather on she feels like a badass. She looks like a badass when she dresses like that and she acts like a badass when she dresses like that. Our appearance determines how we act and how we are treated. If you doubt this, shave your head and dress in a prison uniform for a day and see how it affects your personality and how you are treated. Usually, certain appearances are started by someone in Hollywood or New York that brands an image, and if you want to copy that, you are stereotyping yourself based on the brand of that image.

My family and some friends were at a racing event last month and they were giving out free mohawk haircuts. One of my sons really wanted one. So let's be real. What does a mohawk represent? In most cases, a mohawk represents disobeying authority and rebellion. Hey, I know there are exceptions. We agreed to let him get it if we shaved his head in a few days. It looked really fun on him, but he had to wear a hat in public.

There is a difference between seeking approval from others and not setting my son up for tough times. This little experiment showed the theory of "our appearance equals our attitude" very well. My little boy looked like a rebel and the kiddo acted like a rebel for a few days! That was a reality check. For the record, my son is far from a rebel. I am extremely proud of both of them. "Daddy, can I dye my hair purple?" No!

If I am walking down the streets of Denver at 2:00 a.m. and three guys are leaning up against the wall with hoodies on, covering their faces, it would be wise of me to use my best judgment, get very alert, and cross to the other side of the street. Regardless of their financial status, race, sexual preference or gender, they are representing danger to me. It is very wise for me to listen to that judgment and take action on it. Too many of us get taken advantage of by ignoring the use of our best judgment because we have been programmed to not judge.

I was stuck in this conflicting program for a long time. I am one of those people that for the most part, really do not care what others think. I believe we are all works in progress and if someone is judging me, it is about what they have not accepted about themselves in their own lives. With that being said, I wouldn't always dress as nice as I could have. I didn't spend a ton of time on my fashion appearance or material things. This attitude began to backfire on me. I was having an attitude of, "I'll dress how I want; I don't care what people think. I would rather be rich than look rich."

I learned from others that if I can't even manage my personal appearance, I couldn't expect a partner to trust me to manage a deal. If I don't look the part, I don't get the part. I began to take note. I bought a BMW, Rolex, and began to wear Nordstrom button up shirts. I didn't do it to impress others; I did it because I know the people I do business with are making their decisions about me based on their perception of me. I can't tell you how many deals have come my way just from wearing a Rolex and Bugatchi Uomo shirts. This is a reality of life. People size you up quickly and change their minds slowly. Make it work for you rather than against you.

Never judge based on financial status, race, sexual preference or gender. Always use your best judgment based on the results and choices of those you are considering having an experience with. Appearance is a good indicator of using your best judgment. Always know that your appearance does equal your persuasion and other's perception of you.

Have you heard quitters never win and winners never quit? Generally, I believe this to be true. If we want to accomplish anything in life we need to be one hundred percent committed to it. Are there times when quitting is okay? Yes, absolutely. I prefer to call that redirecting versus quitting, though. A good leader is one that knows when they have made a wrong decision. In cases such as these, they stop and redirect. In other words, don't sink the ship because you are not willing to quit and make a new direction.

If you have committed to a twelve week weight loss program that *you are following*, and after eight weeks you are not getting *any* results, it is time to quit that program and start a different program that may work better. It is time to redirect. It is okay to quit if you recognize that you have made a bad decision or what you committed to is not getting you what you want. However, if quitting affects others that are depending on you, it is vital to honor your commitment and give the ones you are quitting on plenty of notice so that you can be replaced.

As an employer I am shocked when a team member quits with no notice. Although it is very rare, I have been flabbergasted when old team members, who I thought had great character, quit with zero notice. If you told your employer that you would give them a two-week notice if you ever decided to leave, be a person who honors that commitment. Folks, don't do that to the companies you work for. Don't do it to yourself. Unless your employer is unethical, give them notice.

My son wanted to quit his baseball team a couple of years ago. We explained to him that he committed and had to finish out the season. He was upset because he realized he didn't like baseball. We understood; however, his quitting would have affected his team negatively and it also would have taught him that it is okay to quit if you don't like it anymore. Just because you don't like something does not mean that you can quit and not honor your commitment.

Usually, right before we quit something, we feel a large wall of resistance. One of the secrets of life is to commit and push through the resistance. Learn from the experience and continue. If you can push through the resistance and communicate, then you usually don't *want* to quit. Every time you think of quitting, monitor your thoughts and negative charge and find out *why* you want to quit. This is always a great opportunity to grow.

Commitment is doing the thing you said you were going to do long after the mood you were in when you made it is over. It is okay to quit if you realize you have made a wrong decision and you are going to start a new commitment that will help you get what you want. Your time commitment needs to be honored if your quitting is going to affect others negatively.

READY, AIM, FIRE VERSUS READY, FIRE, AIM

This approach is based on how you make decisions. I used to be stuck in *analysis paralysis*. I would be ready and then aim, aim, aim... and never fire. What I found to work best is to be ready, fire, and then aim. Get an idea, go for it, and then correct as you go. I like to call correcting as you go "the moonwalk." Jump in and if you need to back up, keep your head up, moonwalk back, and get back in there a different way!

TO LOVE OR NOT TO LOVE

Have you ever heard that whoever cares the least in the relationship has the most control? I can promise you that program is coming from someone who is not in a very happy relationship. Decide to go all in with no regrets and know that you may experience joy and you may experience hurt, but you will definitely *fully* experience! When you have the chance to love, choose love.

DESIRE VERSUS NOT

If you want to be happy, be grateful with what you have. Does this mean to not desire more? Of course not. Go after your desires. Go after your wants, big time! Do you know how lucky you are to be one of the five percent of human beings that were born in America, a country with opportunity to get everything you have ever wanted? That is a miracle in itself. You live in a country that allows you to be, do, and have most anything you want! God Bless America!

Have you heard that to have no desire or attachment equals no suffering? I guess if your goal is to never suffer then one way to do that is to not go after what you want or be attached to any outcomes. I don't think you would be reading this book if you didn't want to go after what you want, though. What I believe this means is to go after what you want but make sure you are enjoying the process! Commit and do your best to attain it. If you don't get what you wanted, then and only then become unattached. If you did your best and things did not turn out the way you wanted, then let it go. You did your best. Be totally unattached to it. It may not be in the cards right now.

GUARDING YOUR REPUTATION VERSUS SEEKING
APPROVAL OF OTHERS

If you don't give others certainty about who you are and what you are about, they will be stuck in doubt and when someone is stuck in doubt, they create their own certainty about you. Why take that chance? Your reputation is important. Your reputation is your brand. It does need to be guarded. If you have worked hard all of your life and made good choices, you will have a credible, good reputation. If your reputation is messed with, and you didn't have anything to do with it, I believe it should be guarded and defended. If you did have something to do with it, your reputation should be given the chance to be corrected.

Now does this mean that you are seeking approval from others because you care about your reputation? No, it means you are living your life based on your truth, independent of most others' opinions. The difference between guarding your reputation and seeking approval is that when we seek approval, we are really seeking acceptance from others because we have not accepted ourselves fully. Guarding your reputation has nothing to do with seeking acceptance from others. It is about guarding your personal brand to continue to get what you want.

> **Bottom line:** If we have incongruent programs that are causing confusion in our lives, we need to get certain on our programs with clarity. When we are certain, we get what we want.

Chapter Thirteen: Self-leadership

"Champions aren't made in gyms. Champions are made from something they have deep inside them, a desire, a dream, a vision. They have last minute stamina; they have to be a little faster."

-Muhammad Ali

Are you beginning to get clear on who you are, why you're here, and what you want? Are you beginning to see that you can get what you want? I want you to get what you want. Successful people are very clear on who they are, what they want, and how they are going to get it. Most people usually are not clear on who they are, do not know what they want, and do not know where they are going. They are clearer on what they don't want. We are all in the "most people" category at some point in our life. I want to wake everyone up out there that needs to answer these questions.

It takes guts to go after what you want. It takes self-leadership and an ability to lead yourself. Why is it important? Once you lead yourself, you get what you want. Once you master the basic qualities of a leader, you make things happen. All great leaders focus on leading themselves, and if you want to get what you want, you must be able to do this more often than not. Have you ever noticed that everyone you look up to does a better job at leading themselves than you do? It's true. People who get what they want have learned to lead themselves. If they fall down, they get back up and push harder and further.

When you think of a strong leader, what qualities come to mind? Do they include decisiveness, commitment to excellence, and self-disciplined? Are they known for perseverance, vision, and a "do it now" attitude? Do they know to live for the experience and fulfillment, not just the achievement? My guess is they are and they do. Self-leadership is a lifetime process and the book you have in your hands, my friend, will give you one hell of a head start! Growth is always intentional, always. Let's nail down a few of the most important traits as they relate to self-leadership and helping you get what you want.

FOCUS

Self-leadership involves developing a fierce focus to achieve what you want. When I say fierce focus, I mean fierce. People who shine with self-leadership have blocked off times, daily or weekly, to do nothing but focus on what they want and how they are going to get it. They guard this time with everything they have. Folks, everyone and everything around you compete for your time. It must be guarded. During your focus time, consider yourself at war with nasty time suckers. Turn off the cell phone and instant messages. Put up the do not disturb sign and get to work. Consider any interruption in your focus time to be an interruption that is literally taking away your ability to achieve what you want.

Never underestimate the power of focus. Get clear, get focused, and take action. Develop the same kind of focus that you would need if you were attempting to get your head out of water when held beneath the surface. The kind of focus a gazelle has when running from a cheetah. The kind of focus a starving pit bull has when going after a T-bone steak. The kind of focus a pig has when holding on to his bacon. If you want to get what you want, you must focus on it. To be a person of great self-leadership, remember that successful people do what unsuccessful people don't.

COMMITMENT TO EXCELLENCE

You know when you are giving it your all, don't you? Whether it is a project to complete, a test to study for, a workout to push yourself through, a relationship to make work, a child that needs your attention, or even an outfit you are picking out for yourself, you know when you have committed that act to excellence. It shows in the results. If you are going to rake leaves from the yard, it just takes a little more effort to do that project with excellence, doesn't it? It usually takes an extra five minutes to just push through the resistance and complete the job the way it should be done.

A friend of mine loves the quote, "If you don't have time to do it right, when are you going to have time to correct it?" Great quote, isn't it? Go the extra mile, complete the job with pride, and see the results in your life. Half-assed, pardon the term, doesn't get you where you want to go. Half-assed doesn't get the relationships you deserve. There is nothing glorious about being average. Average is the best of the worst and the worst of the best. The *Elevate* mindset is not for the average. Be the person that commits to excellence in everything you do. Check out the video online titled 212 Degrees. It shows Commitment to Excellence and how championship golfers win on average by less than three strokes. Olympic runners win the gold medal by less than a second. Professional racecar drivers have a difference of over half a million dollars in prize money between first and second place. Commit to excellence!

What little thing can you do every day that keeps you committed to excellence? I was getting a smoothie one day, and I accidentally dropped my paper straw cover on the ground. I was talking on my phone with one hand, holding my smoothie with my other hand, and I began to walk out the door. That little voice came in my head and said, "No, no, no, you are committed to excellence, remember?" So needless to say, I put my call on hold and picked it up. What little thing can you do every day that keeps you committed to excellence?

Part of committing to excellence is committing to commitment. Can you imagine what your life would be like if you only did what you *felt* like doing? You would probably be miserable and a huge failure until you snapped out of that mindset. Let's take exercise for example. Do you ever *feel* like exercising? I usually don't. But you are in control of your physiology. You tell your body to get out of bed and hit the gym regardless of how you feel, correct? The first victory of the day is every morning when you beat the battle of the bed! Once you finally get up and begin your exercise, and your body tells you to give up and quit, what do you do? You push through even harder! Make the choice to win every time against your mind. Commit to excellence.

DECISIVE

People who lead themselves are decisive and action oriented. They don't just talk about it, they do it. They know that procrastination is the killer of dreams. They know that if they don't make a decision, they have made a decision. They link a lot of pain to that. They know that if they don't make a decision, a decision will be made for them. They link an extra lot of pain to that! Every decision they make, they are deciding on whether that decision will get them closer or farther to getting what they want long term. They know that every decision they make will direct the course of their life!

The next time you have a decision to make, ask yourself, "Will this decision support me in becoming the best version of myself?" The next time you are going to make a decision regarding exercise, your next meal, the next sentence that comes out of your mouth, or the next dollar you spend, ask yourself if what you are about to do will support you in achieving what you want. If it will, do more of it. If it won't, do less of it. Do you need to make some decisions? Ask yourself if there is anything you need to do more of or less of? Is there anything you need to start doing or stop doing? What decisions do you need to make to get what you want?

Our minds are making decisions every minute of every day. If you don't spend time connecting to God today, how will it affect your life tomorrow? If you eat a greasy hamburger and oily fries today, how will it affect your life tomorrow? If you sleep in and don't exercise today, how will it affect your life tomorrow? If you don't save for your child's college tuition today, how will it affect your life tomorrow? If you only give half of your effort at work today, how will it affect your life tomorrow? People who are good at leading themselves are decisive and they do it now. Do it now. Do it now. Do it now.

Be decisive and have fun doing it. Never make a decision based on fear. Whenever I take advice from fear, I might as well kick myself in my own macadamias. When I take advice from fear, I am dead. Always make a decision based on what you have to gain, not on what you have to lose. Of course, be smart and make sure the risk is calculated, but if we are not getting fearful with some of our big decisions, we are not reaching far enough.

Never make a decision based on fear.

Speaking of being fearful with decisions, I received my Doctor of Chiropractic degree in 1998. I was drawn to chiropractic because of its natural first philosophy and emphasis on health and wellness instead of sick care. I loved the aspect of taking care of the spine and nervous system for health instead of drugging the body for health. I practiced for over ten years and at that point I was really ready to take my career to the next level. I loved being a chiropractor and helped thousands of people; however, that little voice inside me kept saying I was destined for bigger. I was destined for more. At the time I made this decision I had one of the largest single practices in my state. I was making more money than I could imagine and still, I knew I had to take the next step. I begin to transition out and bring on associates so that I could open up other wellness offices and have an even bigger impact on my state and country.

I was scared to do it. I was scared to jump into the uncomfortable zone and risk losing what I had worked so hard to gain. I literally told my wife, "We may have a for sale sign in the front yard soon; however, I must do this. We may be living in your parent's basement," I said, "but

I would rather have the whole world against me than my own soul." It became a must for me. My loving wife supported my decision and it took a few years to get back to financial stability again; however, she has been by my side the entire time and our decision has paid off in more ways than I can imagine.

If you need to make a decision, go for it. Do what you were born to do. Love who you were born to love. Be the person you were meant to be. Have what you were meant to have. Live the life you were meant to live. I want you to get what you want. You need to be the one that not only wants it, but also is willing to make the decision to get it, take action on it, and make it happen.

PERSEVERANCE

As soon as you get the desire to change and make a decision to take action, and practice the disciplines to get what you want, just keep persisting and you will achieve your dreams! Look, we all get beat up from time to time. The key is how fast you bounce back! When I meet a successful, accomplished retired entrepreneur, they always say that the best time they had in business was when they were constantly coming up against struggles and challenges and having to find a way to overcome them. That was their juice! The journey is the juice, folks! If you are having speed bumps in accomplishing what you want, that is awesome! You are going after what you want! You are already destined for greatness. That means you are going to be great. Now it is just a matter of making that happen. It is already set for you. Just keep on listening to the voice inside, keep on making good choices, and keep on going after what you want. I believe in you!

Keep on keeping on! If you are going through hell, don't stop! You can't have a testimony without a test, and you can't have a mission without a mess. If you are ever feeling beat up, that is your body's way of telling you it is time to take a mental break. It is time to get refreshed again. It is time to get inspired again. It is time to focus on why you are pursuing what you want. We all need inspirational fuel on a regular basis. Go get some! Be the person that even though they might fall down seven times, they get up eight! Do whatever it takes, pay any price, travel any distance, do not stop until you achieve what you want. You can do it!

Don't you want to be the person that goes for it? That is an awesome character trait. Be the person that goes for it. You can never build a reputation on what you're going to do, right? You can't become if you only say what you would have done. Give up the excuses. If you are tired of starting over, stop giving up! Excuses are only steps backward from your dream. Life is going to kick you. We all know that. But let it keep kicking you forward! Just keep going back to your desire when you feel this way. Look, it is all about mindset. If you don't have a challenge, how can you have any growth? Pain is going to happen to us all, just keep learning from it, moving forward, keep dreaming, keep taking action, persevere!

What is the farthest you have ever run? If you're anything like me, it took me a long time to realize that if I just *keep going* it gets easier. For years I always heard about the runners high once they got in a good rhythm and cadence. I kept trying to achieve this, but I would stop and never run far enough on my first wind not knowing I was so close to getting my second! Keep going. I actually ran a marathon eventually! Be the little engine that could! Success takes practice and practice makes you better. Keep learning; keep growing. The more you sweat in peace, the less you will bleed in battle! Pain is temporary and pride is forever! Can I get an *Arrrghhh?*

I was at the skate park recently with my sons. They are just starting out and really going for it. So many lessons on perseverance can be taken away from the skate park. We were watching this one kid in particular, who was clearly the most skilled skater there and was trying to land a very difficult trick. He must have fallen ten times and this kid would fall hard! He didn't care what anyone thought. He was pushing himself beyond his comfort zone and learning a new level of mastery. This "kid" became my inspirational teacher for the day. If we don't fall, we are not pushing ourselves hard enough and we are not getting better or closer to getting what we want. Please learn that it is not only okay to fall, but it is desirable! Perseverance is a key.

SELF-DISCIPLINE

Every day we are preparing for success or failure whether we know it or not. I mentioned above that we all will have the pain of challenges. It's true. How we respond to them is what makes it suffering or not. Pain is inevitable; suffering is optional. There are two kinds of pain in life, the pain of discipline and the pain of regret. Which one do you choose?

Let's choose the pain of discipline. Everything comes with a price, and I promise you that the price you pay for failure and giving up on yourself is much more painful than the price of being consistent and taking action to get what you want. Inconsistency is even more painful than consistency. Cement it in your brain that the pain of self-discipline is momentary and the payoff is long lasting. Don't feel like hopping on the treadmill? Hop on for only two minutes and then see how you feel.

Self-discipline is all about deferring immediate gratification in pursuit of a bigger achievement. It is easier to say no to six cream-filled donuts when you have a deeper yes! A fundamental skill is to resist impulse. The way to get better at self-discipline is to know that every choice you make can put you in a better place for the next choice.

Once you know what you want, and how to get it, do it and do it on a regular basis. If you get stuck, go back to the reason you are doing it in the first place. Can I fill you in on a little magic? Okay, do you want to know the secret to consistency, the secret to consistent action to getting what you want? Yes? Yes? Okay. The secret to consistency has two parts. Here we go:

1. Link your highest value to whatever you want to achieve. This is an incredibly motivating secret. Whatever is most important to you, figure out the link on how it will be helped if you get what you want. For example, let's say you are having a hard time losing weight. You have tried everything, blah, blah, blah. Let's say what is most important to you are your kids. How will losing weight help your kids? Get it? Do this now. What are you wanting and what is most important to you? How does getting what you want help what is most important to you? What did you come up with? We will explore this more when we go over getting crystal clear on what you want.

2. Develop your daily actions to get what you want until they become unconscious habits and constant automatic behaviors that help you get what you want. Need more money, make it an unconscious habit to invest ten percent every paycheck without looking at it. Need six pack abs? Make it an unconscious habit to pack your meals every night for the next day. You get the picture.

Bottom line: To get what you want you must be a person committed to leading yourself. The keys to leading yourself are: focus, committing to excellence, making powerful decisions, persevering, and being consistent. The more you lead yourself, the faster you will get what you want.

Elevate

Part Four

The *Elevate* Action: It's Go Time, Baby

Elevate

14 Chapter Fourteen: What do I want?

"If you don't know where you are going,

any road will get you there."

-Lewis Carroll

So what do you want? Really? What do you want? Who do you want to be? What do you want to do? What do you want to have? What kinds of experiences and things do you want in your life? This is awesome. This is what self-growth is all about. This is where being your best, doing your best, and having the best starts. When you can answer the above questions with crystal clear clarity, hang on, because as you know, what you focus on you get! So many of us go through life taking what life gives us. We don't know what we want and never put ourselves on the path to having it all. Life is better in the front row, folks. No more spectating. Get in the driver's seat and make your wants and desires reality. Don't let fear stop you from getting what you want, either! We are going to turn our big desires into big plans! Put yourself out there.

For some of us, we are not sure what we want. That's okay for now; just keep asking questions. What is not working for you in your life? In what area of your life are you detecting negativity? What area are you not having fun in anymore? Let's keep digging until we find out with certainty what it is that we want. Are your relationships not going well? Get certain about what you need from a relationship to be happy. Money challenges? Get certain about what you need to do to secure income. Who can you ask to get help and advice from? Health challenges? Get certain about what you need to do to achieve a long-lasting life of health and vitality. Ask the right questions and certainty becomes yours.

For most of us, we need to get back to elevating the basic areas of our life. Most of us will want improvement in our health, wealth, and relationships. We are going to dive into these categories soon. Don't be afraid to dream big when finding out what it is that you want. John

Elway is one of the best quarterbacks in NFL history. When he was a kid, he knew what he wanted, the NFL. When he was in grade school, he wanted to play in junior high. When he was in junior high, he wanted to play in high school. When he was in high school, he wanted to play in college. When he was in college, he didn't just want to be in the NFL, he wanted to be the best all time quarterback in the world, in the NFL.

When getting clarity on what we want, it's time to dream big. What did you want to be when you grew up? When your dream becomes your reality, your reality becomes your dream. Live your dream. Small plans do not enflame our hearts. Stretch yourself. Get uncomfortable.

My wife and I started out as two kids in the trailer park. While our homes had a lot of love in them, they certainly left desire for material things and experiences. Now don't get me wrong, I knew kids that had the best of the best as far as things and experiences, but no love, and believe me, I would not trade places with them for a second. As we begin to get clear on what we want, remember, a healthy love for God, yourself and others comes first, and then comes better material things and experiences. If you try to go the other way, be careful. It doesn't work and I know you don't want to join the, "those other people" club. I know for a fact that you can have both internal *and* external joy. Just keep the priorities straight, first people, then things.

THE TIME IS NOW

I was having lunch with my sister and nephew downtown one day. It was an inspirational day and the sun was out. I got into a deep conversation with my nephew about what it is that he wants. He is in his mid-twenties and still has not gotten clear on what direction he is headed. The clock is ticking. Can you relate? He has proven himself to be responsible, good at taking risks, and good at pushing forward through resistance. While I was listening to him, it was obvious that he had what it takes to be successful in all areas of his life. He represented to me how many people out there have many of the basic fundamentals down, but just haven't made a decision on which way to go. After our lunch I could see that he was ready to make

Indecision is insanity. Don't wait for years and years to finally figure out what path you want to get on to get what you want.

some decisions. I was proud of him. If you are in this boat, it does not stop until you make the decision on which direction you want to go!

Indecision is insanity. Don't wait for years and years to finally figure out what path you want to get on to get what you want.

Look, just make the decision. Be the ready, fire, aim person. Once you have made the decision, expect the best and accept the worst-case scenario if the decision you make ends up being a wrong one. You will learn from every decision you make, so it is hard to even call any decision a wrong one. However, if you feel you did make the wrong decision, remember, do the moonwalk, back up and correct it or change it. Learn from it and move forward. Don't let indecision on deciding what it is that you want take up any more of your precious life. Your heart only gets so many beats.

Is your age keeping you from going for it? If it is, this is for you. The average working adult works from age twenty to sixty years old, about forty years. Let's break up forty years into four quarters. At age thirty, you just finished first quarter. You have plenty of time to make it happen. At age forty, consider that half time. You still have twenty more years to make it happen! At age fifty, consider that fourth quarter. You still have ten more years to make it happen, and most of the world's best comebacks happen in the fourth quarter! If you are under age twenty and reading this book, then you are probably already a billionaire or on your way to being one, and I look forward to learning from you! If you are sixty years old or older, that is called overtime. Never give up. God is counting on all of us to get clear on what we want so we can contribute to our world with the gifts we have been given. Don't be the one that lives life in quiet desperation. Don't be the one that wishes they had done more with the gifts they had been given. Do it and do it now.

What we all want is happiness. Everything that you *want* is to make you happy. Personally, for me to be completely internally filled with joy and happiness, it stems from my relationship with God. We have already discussed spirituality in detail, so I urge you if you are not at peace in this area, then ask the people you need to ask to get at peace in this area. In my opinion, a spiritual relationship with your creator is a must for internal joy. The other areas in our life that will make us happy the fastest tend to revolve around our health, wealth, and relationships.

ACTION JACKSON

Think about a moment you had roughly twelve months ago. Take Thanksgiving, for example. Can you remember your last Thanksgiving holiday? How about the one before that? When you can think of a moment you had about a year ago, continue reading. How long ago does that memory seem? Like last week, right? It blows me away to talk about events that happened about twelve months ago and realize that was a year ago! A year ago! Time does not stop! Just think, if you had taken action on what you wanted one year ago, it would have already been a year now! For example, have you been thinking of going back to school for a while? If you had started a year ago, you would have already completed your first year! This little tool is a great motivator on taking action now! Can you imagine how you would look and feel now if you had started and remained consistent on your health and fitness plan one year ago? A year from now, you will wish you had started going after what you wanted today!

Start with a dream. Put reality to it and make it a crystal clear vision, and then set up goals toward your vision. When your purpose is at the base of all of it, it is impossible to fail. Success to me is actively pursuing your dreams. It has nothing to do with the end accomplishment. It has everything to do with being happy and fulfilled as you go after what you want. The accomplishment will be fantastic, but the moment you are going after what you want, in my eyes, you are successful. Once you know what you want, take a small step toward it immediately!

We have been building up to deciding what it is that we want. I know by now you know generally what it is that you want. Let's now make it crystal clear. We are going to decide what it is that we want. If you don't get clear on what you want, you won't take action. Why do the words consistency, determination, perseverance, and commitment bring on a sudden feeling of pain for most of us? Because it's incredibly hard to follow through on our goals, that's why! Life gets in the way, right?

So many times we have started toward a desire that was super important to us only to let it slip away from contributing to our greatness. Our victorious goals in our minds soon become defeats. They become jaded thoughts and painful memories telling us, why bother again? They become our boo hoos. Can you relate? Seriously, it is not easy to follow through on what we commit to. How do we break the cycle of not following through on goals we set for ourselves? Here's how.

This is a five-part approach that will change your life, folks. I call it the Five-Step Action Jackson. It's not only a formula, but a dance! Check out the dance at www.ElevateBook.com/Bonus.

Let's start with the formula:

1. Determine what you want and set your goal.

2. Have an incredibly strong WHY with massive pleasure and pain.

3. Take action on what you need to do to make it happen.

4. Visualize and affirm your goal.

5. Give and get massive support.

We are going to explore each of these; however, I'm telling you, this is the answer you have been waiting for. It is simple, but not easy. I will show you how to get it done. We are going to start with deciding on what it is that we want.

DECISION TIME

Let's start with our health, wealth, and relationships. I'm still guessing that whatever you want the most, will probably fit in one of these categories. The next chapters really dive into best practices and habits of success for each of these areas if you do not know *how* to get what you want. For now, get clear on *what* you want in each area and by what date you want it. Drum roll please; the buck stops here. Right here, right now! Today is a new day, a new thought process, a new beginning! I'm feeling it. You feeling it? Let's do this! Okay? Okay, let's do it now. Ready, Set, Go!

HEALTH:

So what are your health wants? Do you want to command more respect and attract more success with a stronger, leaner, more energized body? Are you too fat? Are you too skinny? Do you get sick a lot? Are you in pain? Are you fatigued? What do you want for your health? How do you want to feel? What changes do you need to make in your health life to be happy? Here are some examples.

General: I want to feel sexy and vibrant. I want tons of energy. I want to limit my alcohol intake. I want to look lean. I want thicker hair. I want to discontinue my use of toxic substances.

Specific: I want to release thirty pounds of fat. I want to gain ten pounds of muscle. I want to get off all of my medications. I want to eat organic protein and produce. I want to get a weekly adjustment and massage. I want to meditate daily. I want to quit all use of tobacco.

Let's do it. What do you want to start doing, stop doing, do less of or do more of in the health category of your life? Do you have it? When you are ready, let's now make what you want a goal.

HEALTH GOAL

1. What do I want?
2. Is what I want specific and measureable?
3. When do I want to complete it?

WEALTH

So what are your wealth wants? Are you too poor? Do you have too much money and do not know what to do with it all? Are you behind on your bills? Are you in financial pain? Are you at a job that you hate that you stay at just to pay the bills? Do you want to learn how to invest? What changes do you need to make in your wealth life to be happy? Here are some examples.

General: I want to feel rich and financially secure. I want tons of money. I want to limit my spending. I want to have fewer bills. I want to learn to invest.

Specific: I want to begin my investment plan by the first of the month. I want to save ten percent of my income. I want to discontinue my use of all of my department store credit cards. I want to reduce my monthly budget by twenty percent. I want to have a weekly phone conference with my financial advisor.

Let's do it. What do you want to start doing, stop doing, do less of or do more of in the wealth category of your life? Do you have it? When you are ready, let's now make what you want a goal.

WEALTH GOAL

1. What do I want?
2. Is what I want specific and measureable?
3. When do I want to complete it?

So what are your relationship wants? Are you stressed out with your spouse or children? Is your communication poor? Do you experience pain in your relationships? Do you want to have an incredible relationship with your spouse? Do you want to make friends with others that have higher standards than yours? What changes do you need to make in your relationship life to be happy?

General: I want to feel loved. I want an awesome relationship with my spouse. I want to limit my exposure to some friends. I want to spend more time with my kids.

Specific: I want to limit my exposure and end my relationship with my friend that keeps pulling me down by the end of the month. I want to visit with a new friend who is more successful than I am, once a month. I want to stop ignoring my kids. I want to play with my children individually once a day. I want to begin a weekly date night with my spouse. I want to pray with my wife every night.

Let's do it. What do you want to start doing, stop doing, do less of or do more of in the relationship category of your life? Do you have it? When you are ready, let's now make what you want a goal.

RELATIONSHIP GOAL

1. What do I want?

2. Is what I want specific and measureable?

3. When do I want to complete it?

ACTION JACKSON EXPANDED

So you now know what you want. Woo hoo! You have made what you want a goal by making it specific and measureable and with a deadline. Now let's set you up with determining why you want it and how you are going to get it. So take one goal you decided on from each category and apply the Five-Step Action Jackson formula to each one.

FIVE-STEP ACTION JACKSON

1. Determine what you want. Ask yourself what you want more of, less of, want to start doing, or stop doing altogether? Make it specific, attainable, and with a deadline. What is your goal?

2. Have an incredibly strong WHY with massive pleasure and pain. You know yourself better than anyone. Which sentence do you respond better to?

    Stop eating greasy hamburgers more than once a week or you will die an early painful death, disappointing everyone who loves and depends on you.

    OR

    Stop eating greasy hamburgers more than once a week so you can live a long wonderful life spending time with everyone you love.

    Both work. You may not like the questions, especially if you love greasy hamburgers; however, the purpose is to see if you are motivated by the promise of future pain, or the promise of future pleasure. Which one motivates you more? I recommend using both. Once you recognize your future benefits and future consequences, write down how getting your goal will positively affect your life and how not getting your goal will negatively affect your life. How will achieving your goal affect the most important areas of your life? Why do you want to achieve your goal? Remember, these are benefits you will achieve by reaching your goal and the negative consequences if you do not. Make sure your WHYs are linked to your highest values. For example: God, Health, Wealth, and Relationships. You need to really feel the weight of your WHY.

3. Review your physical action plan. What is your strategy for accomplishing your goal? What do you need to do physically to make this happen? What daily habits do you need to create to get what you want? The first key is to know how to do it right. Find someone who has accomplished what you want to accomplish and do what they do with no tweaks! Get help on this one. If you knew how to do it right, you wouldn't be where you are now, right?

    Remember, knowledge is demonstrated by results, not intellect.

Find a book, an audio, a coach, or a professional that knows how to accomplish what you want. If looking for a professional to help with your action plan, make sure they walk the talk. Remember, knowledge is demonstrated by results, not intellect. If someone is going to tell you how to do it, make sure that they are a person that takes action on what they know how to do. Knowing what to do and actually doing it are worlds apart. You deserve the whole package.

If you want to lose weight, your trainer needs to be fit. If you want to make more money, your advisor needs to have more money than you do. If you really take this to heart, your options will become very, very clear. Only take advice from people that you want to be like in that area. The next three chapters will help you form your action plan if you need it. What is your action plan to get what you want? Your physical action plan will soon become habits that you do not have to think about.

4. Visualize and affirm your goal. This is your key to taking physical action and getting the results you want. Visualize your completed goal and how it feels. Look at a picture that motivates you. Really feel it. Read affirmations specific to your goal. Affirmations are quotes that are specific to the category of your goal and contain common sense wisdom. They are easily found online. If your goal is pertaining to health and fitness, for example, do a search for health and fitness affirmations.

5. Give and get massive support. People who join or create support groups get much better results. I didn't know how important this was until I tried it. It works. Create a group you can meet with or touch base with once a week. They become your accountability group. Your support group is counting on you. It's powerful to join a group where everyone has the same goal. Just make sure that the leader of the group has accomplished what you want. If this is not an option, have a couple of friends that you know want what is best for you and are happy to support you. Don't choose a friend that will be "okay" if you start to slip. You want a friend that will be strong enough to get you back on track.

That is the Five-Step Action Jackson! Review these five steps every day! You can apply this in less than two minutes a day when you wake up and before you go to bed. Do this and your dreams will become your reality.

When it comes to the words consistency, determination, perseverance, and commitment, all you are asking yourself for is to review your five steps in less than two minutes, twice a day. You've got this! This is the key you have been waiting for. I know you have what it takes to stick with this. Go after what you want. You matter, and I love you as a person! If you have not yet seen the video for this chapter, I suggest you check it out now at www.ElevateBook.com/ Bonus. Watch the dance; hear the song. Listen to it three times and you will be singing it all day!

REVIEW TWICE A DAY

1. Know what you want.
2. Know why you want it.
3. Work your plan.
4. See your results.
5. Give and get support.

RESULT: Achieve what you want! Achieve what you want! Achieve what you want!

VISION VERSUS GOALS VERSUS HABITS

It can get a little confusing to talk about wants and visions and goals and habits. Let's clarify what these are. A *vision* is what you want to ultimately be, do, and have. A *goal* is a specific measureable achievement with a deadline to eventually achieve your ultimate vision. A *habit* is a small action that you do on a daily basis to achieve your goal and to ultimately achieve your vision. Think of your vision as your ultimate achievement, and when and if you achieve it, you can die knowing you gave it your all and you went toward your vision. Your goals are the smaller steps you had to continually make and complete to get you closer to your vision. Your habits are the daily routines and action steps you created to hit your goals and ultimately your vision.

FEAR AND COURAGE

It can be scary to go after what you want. It is supposed to be. You want to feel uncomfortable and put yourself out there to get what you really, really want. If it was not uncomfortable for you, you would already have it. The reason fear kicks in is because it is supposed to! This is normal. This is your indicator that says that you *are* reaching far enough.

I do not believe fear can be totally avoided; however, it can be greatly minimized by how we mentally set up the decisions we make before we process them. If we train our minds to have a positive expectation instead of a negative expectation, we can eliminate a lot of fear. If you think, "My husband is going to get really upset if I tell him I want our kids to go to private school," then you will produce some fear. This is a negative expectation, and negative expectations produce fear. If you think, "My husband is going to be really excited about our kid's education and future by placing them on a track that will help them succeed faster," then you will produce excitement through positive expectation. Give it a shot. Begin to program your mind to expect acccptance and excitement, not rejection.

Now regardless of how positive our expectations are, we still can battle with fear. The key is to recognize it and smash it. Have you ever heard of a Mulaheenie? I made the word up, but it's fun to say! A Mulaheenie is an ancient warrior whose job is to keep you from getting your dreams. He is that negative voice in your head that squashes every dream you have when you begin to feel uncomfortable about going for something you want! You say, "I want to have rock hard abs and buns of steel!" The Mulaheenie says, "Never! Don't do it! You will fail just like last time! You are a loser!" When you recognize that voice, destroy it and take action anyway. Kill the monster when it is little! Mentally picture smacking it on the head with a shovel. It works! Sayōnara, sucka!

When fear kicks in, and it is keeping you from moving forward, just take the first step toward your fear and it quickly goes away. As soon as you confront it and push toward it, it goes away. Remember, be a person that is willing to experience anything. Be the person that grabs life, refuses to live in quiet desperation, and goes for it! The more you step up to fear, the fewer things you will have in your life that you are afraid of. Now obviously, make sure you recognize the difference between "false" fear in your head and "real" fear which represents physical danger. Fear representing physical danger is there to protect us and is not to be mistaken for "false" fear which holds us back.

You need to step out to get to where you want to go.

Fear is no laughing matter. I know I am having a little fun with it, but seriously, fear is your enemy if you let it keep you from going after what you want. Too many people need what you can provide. Be the example and help others by conquering fear. Breaking through fear is a fundamental pillar of self-growth that must be accomplished to get what you want. Take the voice of fear very, very seriously and make sure you win more times than not!

Think of all of the opportunities you have missed because you were afraid to say or do something. Opportunities are never missed, by the way, they are simply taken by somebody else. Think of all the people that could have benefitted by your stepping up, and you chose to lose to fear? So much is lost in this world by having a lack of courage. Look, you can't be courageous or brave if you're not scared! Step up to what you want. All the fruit is out on the limb, folks.

You need to step out to get to where you want to go. Break your shackles of inhibition! Screw inhibition! Go after what you want! Create your incredible life by operating from strength and courage, not fear. Don't be the person that misses one hundred percent of the shots they don't take. Life really is much more fun when you say yes instead of no. See the opportunities in every difficulty and know that as soon as you commit to action, regardless of fear, your courage will follow. I promise!

TIME TO STEP UP

Several years ago, my wife and kids and I were driving back from a day of "fun in the sun" at the Boulder Reservoir. We took a different drive home and we came upon this amazing neighborhood. It looked like the average house was about four million dollars. We thought for sure the neighborhood would be gated. To our surprise, it was not gated and we drove through! Here we were, attempting to be incognito in our black Hummer, driving through this highly affluent neighborhood. Our jaws were dropped at the sight of such beautiful homes. We were in dreamland for sure.

As I was driving through, a guy about my age waved me over. I thought, "Oh, shnikes! Busted." It must have been obvious we were driving around because he asked if we were looking for a home to purchase. His was for sale. We told him we were just driving through, dreaming. He seemed like a nice guy and started asking us about our Hummer. We talked for a couple of minutes and were on our way.

We couldn't help but think about how he was able to achieve a beautiful home at such a young age. As we drove away, my wife and I were sparked again to believe what was possible for us. We pulled into our garage and my wife encouraged me to go back and officially meet him. My first thought was fear, and my second thought was courage. That was a great idea. If I wanted to go to the next level, I had to get in the company of people who were already there. Right there, I put in my phone calendar for the following week, "Meet rich guy in nice neighborhood."

Sure enough, a week came and my calendar date to, "Meet rich guy in nice neighborhood" popped up. I piled up my family and made the drive to his house. I wasn't sure if he would remember me or not, but why not? Success involves risk. Success involves putting yourself out there. Success involves commitment.

I parked at the end of the huge circular driveway, told my wife and kids I would be right back, and made the long walk toward the biggest pair of front doors I had ever seen. I lifted up the doorknocker and knocked three times, "Boom, boom, boom." I still wasn't sure what I was going to say, but I knew the commitment was made and it was go time. As I heard the boom of the door, I wasn't sure if I was hearing the sound of my pounding heart or the actual door knock. Regardless, I was drowning out the voice of fear by the sound of my pounding heart!

He opened the door and obviously didn't know who I was. It was time to go for it. I said, "Hi, I met you last week driving through the neighborhood. I don't mean to just walk up like this; however, you seemed like a very approachable nice guy. My wife and I would like to live in a neighborhood like this someday and I thought we may be able to invite you and your wife out to dinner to get to know you a little bit." My heart was still pounding. After a brief pause, he looked down the driveway and saw my family. He said, "Is that your family in the Hummer?" I said, "Yes." He said, "Pull on up and come on in." I said, "Great!"

I felt like I had just won the lottery! I turned around with the biggest smile on my face you can imagine and made my way back to my family. My wife said, "What did he say?" I said, "He said come on in!" She said, "Seriously? Okay, let's go." We went in and got a tour of his magnificent home. He introduced us to his kids, which were the same age as both of ours. He asked if we liked wine, and of course, we both said simultaneously, "Sure!" He pulled out a bottle of wine from his two-story wine cellar. It was a 1975 Merlot. He poured us each a glass and said, "This is about a five hundred dollar bottle of wine." We were so elated, my wife and I started to giggle. The wine was amazing, by the way.

His wife came home shortly thereafter and we also got to meet her. We talked as our kids played, and he said, "You know, I did the same thing to a guy while I was out in France. I walked up to his mansion in the middle of the orchard and introduced myself." Ahhh. He recognized the courage in me.

We ended up taking him and his wife out to a nice steak dinner, shared a meal, a bottle of wine, and listened to his story. He started with nothing and made it happen through real estate and business. With similar backgrounds, the friendship was set! Since meeting my new friend several years ago, we have done many business deals together, formed a good friendship, and have many more deals to come.

Bottom line: You can get what you want in every area of your life. The time is now. Conquer your fears, apply the formulas, and take action!

Chapter Fifteen:
The Habits of Health

"Health and Fitness are the platforms the rest of my life sits on. When I am strong physically, I am strong in every factor of my life."

-Jillian Michaels

Why health? Because if you are dead, you can't really achieve a life of greatness, that's why. Is that right or right? Okay, let's start with what health is. The World Health Organization defines health as "a state of complete physical, mental, and social well-being and not merely the absence of disease or infirmity." They have it right. You have already endured a few of my rant and raves about our current model of health care and how it is not working. In summary, taking drugs called prescriptions to cover up warning signals in our body, called symptoms, is a good way to stay sick, unhealthy, and die early. Now if that motivated you, don't take yourself off of your medications! That is why you have your medical doctor. Let them do that for you.

Your body can self-heal and self-regulate when given the right opportunity. Not taking care of the source of our vitality will eventually cause symptoms. The five keys to elevate your health are: 1) Drastically Reduce Toxins 2) Remove Undetected Nerve Damage 3) Eat Right, 4) Exercise, and, 5) Live the *Elevate* Mindset. I am going to touch on these topics; however, if you need help in diving into these five areas deeper, visit www.discoverhealthandwellness.com and we can help get you where you need to go. Let's take a look at these five areas and get you on the right health track.

DRASTICALLY REDUCE TOXINS

Anything that can cause pathology in your body is a toxin. We are bombarded by thousands of toxins every day. They exist in everything from the air we breathe (dioxins, ozone, carbon monoxide), to the food and drinks we consume. There are toxins such as phylates and BPA that come directly from the plastics and cans that contain our food and drinks. There are herbicides and pesticides sprayed onto our vegetables and fresh fruit. These chemicals and many more have been linked to cancer, birth defects, and autoimmune diseases such as diabetes, lupus, and multiple sclerosis.[10] These toxins are stored in the body's fat cells and can be difficult to extract on our own. There are a variety of toxicity cleanses out there that will cleanse your body and allow it to begin to heal itself.

The best way to get rid of toxins is to go through a supplemental detox diet for a few days and then avoid them as much as possible. Some of the biggest sources of toxins that can be avoided are: unnecessary medications, artificial sweeteners, nonorganic produce and meat, unfiltered water, toxins in our hygiene products, heavy metal toxins in our kitchen pots and pans, most plastics we eat from, and toxic chemicals from the poor lifestyle habits such as excessive alcohol and tobacco use that are known to cause early death. Unfortunately, I know how hard tobacco use is to kick. I picked up the habit of smokeless tobacco in high school and continued for about fifteen years. It is hard to quit, but you can do it. I can relate. Nicotine is not your friend.

Most toxins can be avoided. This list is a summary of the big ones; however, please know that it is impossible to avoid all toxins and that there are still many more to avoid that are not listed here. Do your best with this list and make your new health plan about creating health and wellness, not fighting sickness. To make this jump is a big one. The best way to do it is in steps. I suggest doing the following in any order you wish.

1. Talk to your medical doctor about getting you off of your medications as much as possible. If you are ready to make some lifestyle changes, your medical doctor will be open to it.

2. Only buy your food and hygiene products at natural grocers. I know this is more expensive, but it is less expensive than cancer. Start slow, create the need for it, and your money will begin to flow there. You will feel better!

3. Get a water filter for your home or at least drinking water. A reverse osmosis water system is an inexpensive system you can get set up at your kitchen faucet. Hardware stores carry them. Home water filtration systems are more expensive but they usually have affordable payment plans if necessary.

4. Replace your cookware with stainless steel cookware. Begin to use coconut oil to cook with and you will be amazed how easy stainless steel is to clean. Get rid of all of your plastic and

replace your water bottles or food storage containers with stainless steel or glass ones.

5. Avoid consistent poor lifestyle choices that will eventually kill you. If you are taking, inhaling, or ingesting, something toxic that is destroying your health, seek out a cessation program. You know what you need to do. You deserve it for yourself and those around you to get this one handled. Your body is your vehicle system for life. It is the body in which you experience the world. Make it top notch by not polluting it. Would you let your million-dollar race horse ingest junk all of the time with no moderation? You are worth more than a million dollars, my amigo.

REMOVE UNDETECTED NERVE DAMAGE

As a chiropractor, I know some love us and some not so much. Unfortunately, only about ten percent of the population visit chiropractors. This is due to so much misinformation out there about what it is that we do. My profession has been riddled with myths, fallacies, and even prejudice. If more people knew what we did versus what they thought we did, less people would suffer. But the tide has certainly changed as our population has gotten sicker and sicker. Most people are wise enough now to know that the body is pretty damn smart, and if it is eliciting a symptom, it is asking for help. It is asking for you to find the source of what is causing the symptom. Well, that is what chiropractors do. We find the source of your symptom. If there is pressure and tension on your nervous system, the function of that nerve decreases, and as a result, the function of the organs and organ systems decrease. This causes symptoms in the body. If it cannot be taken care of naturally through adjustments and spinal corrections, that's when we refer to our medical friends.

Do you think it is a good idea to have a strong immune system? With one out of three Americans eventually developing cancer, I think it is important to elevate our immune system as much as possible. A study was performed back in 1987 showing the positive impact that wellness chiropractic care had on the immune system. The study measured one group that had not received chiropractic care and compared their immune system to another group that had received wellness chiropractic care. They found that the group receiving wellness chiropractic care had a two hundred percent stronger immune system than the non-chiropractic group. An oncologist took the study further and compared the chiropractic group to his cancer patients and revealed that the chiropractic group had a four hundred percent stronger immune system than his cancer patients.[11] If I offered you a shot that was toxin free that boosted your immune system by two hundred percent and it fought against cancer, allergies, asthma, influenza, and common colds, would you take it?

Correct posture and spinal correction takes the pressure and tension off of your nervous system, which controls everything. It prolongs your life and the life of your spine. It's time to check out chiropractic for the first time, or again. I can help with that. I happen to know some great ones.

EAT RIGHT AND EXERCISE

Being fit makes you more popular and more attractive to the opposite sex, helps you live longer, and helps you deal with stress more effectively. If you take care of your body, your body will take care of you. We must link our health to our future. Our future is where we are going to spend the rest of our lives. Let's get there in vitality. Great health does not just happen. It needs constant attention. Exercise, for example, makes you think clearer, boosts your confidence, allows you to be more productive and helps you accomplish your dreams faster! Nutrition is all about making conscious decisions on what we put in our mouth. You can eat yourself to pain, suffering, and early death or you can eat yourself to longevity, vibrancy, and vitality! Whenever you are about to eat something, ask yourself, if I eat this now, what do I have to give up later? If you are okay with the answer, then eat it. If you are not okay with the answer and you still really want it, picture maggots and crap on it! Yes, I just wrote that. It works! If you still want it, then you are one sick puppy. Do ten jumping jacks or pushups and walk away. Remind yourself why you are worth your sexy self! If you want to get what you want, know that your health is number one.

Great health does not just happen. It needs constant attention.

Get committed to the body you deserve. You are the one who is in control. Attack poor nutritional or exercise habits as if they are the enemy. When you get that voice in your head that says, "Eat the greasy French fries," recognize it as a voice of an enemy that does not want you to get what you want.

There is so much information out there on exercise and nutrition. The last thing I want to do is confuse the topics even more. I must admit that nutrition and fitness have been my biggest challenge in self-growth. I can personally share the struggle with anyone out there who finds it challenging to stay fit. I am your friend along the path that will openly and honestly say to you, me too! Although this has been one of my greater challenges, I never stop going after it, and I do have what I do down solid.

This is what has worked for me. I have three meals a day and three snacks a day. My portions include fifty percent of my plate as vegetables, a palm-size serving of protein, a little bit of fruit or legumes and some healthy fat, such as olive oil, nuts or avocado. Most people I know that are lean and vibrant avoid unhealthy grains, fried foods, and sugar. I plan two free meals a week in which I allow myself to eat whatever I want. I exercise six days a week, three days resistance training and three days cardio.

THE ELEVATE MINDSET

This entire book has been about the *Elevate* mindset. If I was to sum up the *Elevate* mindset in three points in regards to its impact on your health, to your stress levels, they would be:

1. Know that the big picture is to practice love toward God, ourselves and others. Treat people the way you would like to be treated and know that we really can see the change when we *become* the change.

2. Take one hundred percent responsibility for your life. If something isn't going right for you, ask what you are doing to cause that. This keeps you in control of everything you can control.

3. When you feel stressed, don't stay there. Admit to yourself that what stress really is, is uncertainty, fear, and lack of preparation. If you can change it, do it. If you cannot, accept that everything is going to turn out for the best even though you might not understand it at the moment. Everything that is happening to you is an opportunity to grow as a person.

TOP FIVE HABITS OF HEALTH

If you could you put your entire health plan into five easy habits, and stick to them, and you could have the body, health and vitality of your dreams, would you want to learn them? Me too! Make the following five habits part of your daily life and six pack abs will be yours. Here you go! Always have a specific health target goal and review the Five-

Step Action Jackson every day for that goal. When you hit that goal, make a new one.

1. Avoid toxins: Talk to your medical doctor about avoiding medications whenever possible and only shop for your hygiene and food products at natural grocers. Cook with stainless steel and drink filtered water.

2. Get a wellness chiropractic adjustment and massage regularly.

3. Eat right. Drink a green drink daily and take a multivitamin, vitamin D3, and fish oil supplements. Mainly eat vegetables, protein, a little fruit or legumes, and healthy fats. Avoid unhealthy grains, fried foods, and sugar, and plan two free meals a week to eat whatever you want! Plan and prepare your nutrition, supplementation, and exercise for the next day nightly.

4. Exercise: Work out six days a week for at least twenty minutes—three cardio and three resistance exercises.

5. Practice the *Elevate* mindset: Practice love, take one hundred percent responsibility, and don't allow yourself to stay in a stressful state.

Bottom line: Your health is your responsibility. Everything you love about your life is linked to your health. You deserve energy, vitality, and longevity. You deserve to look and feel your best. You now have the essential tools on how to make that happen. Take action today.

Chapter Sixteen:
The Habits of Wealth

"Money was never a big motivation for me, except as a way to keep score. The real excitement is playing the game."

-Donald Trump

Why wealth? Because if you are poor it is very difficult to focus on anything else but surviving and paying your bills, that's why. You're destined for more than that. Is that right or right? Okay, let's start with what wealth is. Wealth is the subject of money and money accumulation. Money has always been a fun subject for me. I think for most entrepreneurs it usually is. What is money? Seriously, have you ever considered that question? Is money evil? Is money good? What is this little piece of paper with a dead president on it that we call money and why is there so much emotion toward it? I know for some the very mention of money begins to trigger all kinds of nonproductive programs. "I don't need money. Money is not important to me. Why do we have to focus on money? Money is all about greed." If this is you, please keep reading. Saying you don't care about money is like saying you don't care about food, or clothes, or a roof over your head. Money is very, very important.

If you have ever struggled with money, like I did for a long time, this section will be worth its weight in gold. For many of us, the only reason we have struggled with money is because of our negative emotion toward it that came from what we were taught about it. It may have come from people using money in a negative way and now we link all money to negativity. Let's clear this topic up because if one of the things you want is more money, than we must feel good about what money represents. If you were to ask me if I loved money, as my friend Jon says, "If you are talking about little pieces of paper with dead presidents on them, then no, I do not love money. If you are talking about what money represents, then absolutely yes. I love what money represents."

Money represents the byproducts of our services and products! The amount of money you make is a direct reflection to the amount of service you provide to the marketplace. The more service you provide, the more money you make. Do you see that? Money is the result of our proudest accomplishments, service, and products that contribute to our world. If you want more money, stop thinking about money and instead start thinking about ways you can create as much *value* as you can for as many people as you can.

ECONOMICS

So what are your thoughts regarding economics? There are many ways we could go here. How we feel about economics is definitely a huge divider for our relationships and our country. I have recently become more passionate about this topic as I learn about different mindsets regarding it. The best way I know how to share how I feel about economics is by my own story. As you read earlier, I was raised poor, big time. My mom loved me with all of her heart; however, money was certainly not in abundance. She did the best she could at the time with the tools she had, and for that, I will always be grateful. Although I went through the pain as a child of constantly moving and waiting until payday or food stamps to go grocery shopping, these experiences ended up being a wonderful gift in my life as I got older. They made me compassionate for my fellow man who has not been given the opportunity of the lesson of self-responsibility yet.

I was taught the entitlement mentality. I was taught that it is the responsibility of rich people to pay for poor people. I was taught to expect someone who makes more money than me to pay the bill at a restaurant or pitch in more money for an activity. Well, I will be the first one to tell you, this way of thinking did not work for me very well as life went on. This way of thinking was the opposite of taking self-responsibility. This way of thinking was the opposite of being responsible for my choices.

As I grew older, I began to see how our choices affect our income. I saw how most poor people made choices, and I saw how most people with money made choices. I learned quickly that the best way to help the poor is to not be one of them. I decided that I wanted to be rich. I decided that my future kids would be raised in a financially stable home and get to go to Disneyland! I decided that I would make choices in my life that would support me in my desire to get what I want.

Now that I'm an adult, I look back at the choices I made and it worked out. So far, so good! I wish I had made all of the right choices but that is not how life works. I looked at the choices some of my friends made, and for some of them, so far, not so good. My maturity taught me that if I want to *have* more, *I am the one* that needs to make that happen.

As I grew through my early years, I learned that I was the one that needed to avoid drugs, hang out with eagles, take responsibility for my life, go to college, practice safe sex in a committed relationship, save my money, and provide service to the world and get paid for it. I knew that the more I stuck to these choices, the better off I would become. I learned quickly that people who make the right choices have and deserve more than people who make the wrong choices. As obvious as this may or may not sound to you, until we know that our choices are our responsibility, and that our choices determine what we get in life, we just don't know.

PORK CHOPS

So what is money? Money is simply a tool of exchange. It was invented for our convenience. It was invented so we could get pork chops easier. I'll explain. Once upon a time, long, long ago in a land far, far away, you were awoken early one fine beautiful morning to the ruckus of your five kids playing by the hot stove. "Daddy, Daddy, we want pork chops tonight for dinner! We are so hungry for some yummy pork chops!" You crawl out of bed and put on your suspenders. You want to be a good daddy that fills his kid's bellies up with yummy pork chops. You let your family know that you are going to the country market and will be back in a few hours.

You gather up ten chickens from the coop and head on down to the market. One of the chickens gets out of the cage and it takes you another hour to finally catch that rascal. You get to the market and begin to talk to several people and see if they would like to trade your ten chickens for two goats. You finally find someone who needs ten chickens and is willing to trade you their two goats. Now you need to find someone who wants your two goats for one fat pig with juicy pork chops. You're tired, so you take a little break and gather up more gumption to find your next trade. Finally! You find a little old grandma that wants to trade her fat pig for your two goats. You make the trade, get the greasy pig home and off to the slaughter shed you go. At 6:00 pm that night, you are the Daddy of the Year and your family gets their fat, juicy pork chops. Yummmmm. Do you see now why money was made because of pork chops? I guess that is why I have always been fond of pigs. Bring on the bacon, baby.

Now instead of trading livestock, we can go to the market and pay money for what we want. Money is a tool of exchange, nothing more, nothing less. Every emotion, every experience, and every example we have that turns money into anything else other than a tool of exchange is false. Inventing money gave us convenience and the ability to store

163

wealth. I no longer have to have a huge herd of cattle and wheat for wealth. Now I just need a bank account with money in it. Get it? Got it? Good!

BUSINESS

One of my first jobs was at a grocery store, and we had a required union to join. I remember when we were getting ready to go on our first strike. Here I was, sixteen years old, a bagger at a grocery store, and seeing adults all around me talk about how they were not paid enough. I couldn't grasp it. My thought was, "You knew how much the job paid; you made the choice to work here; and now that you do work here, you want more money, but do not want to work more?" That doesn't make any sense. The employees at the time that were the biggest advocates for the strike were quite honestly, the least productive employees and the biggest complainers. At sixteen years old, I was watching adults have the opportunity to get hired and receive a mutually agreed upon wage, and now expect the owner of the grocery store to pay them more for not doing any more production.

This was a lesson learned. I learned right there that the employees that got paid the most provided the most value to their companies. I do understand that unions are formed to protect the employees of the companies and management they work for. I guess I have just never worked for a company that didn't reward the employees that were productive and weren't fair in their management decisions.

Look, companies need to be responsible to their employees. They need to pay a good wage for good workers. They need to take care of the most important people in their organization, the productive employees! As a small business owner myself, if this doesn't happen, you just don't keep good employees. I think where many of us get divided is when we automatically think of big corporations as being evil and greedy. Most large companies started with one person with a dream. It started with one person willing to put up their homes as collateral to the bank, take one hundred percent responsibility, work as hard as they possibly could, provide a ton of jobs for their fellow man, and provide a service or product to the world that society was willing to pay for. The more value a corporation

If you work for a company and you are not appreciated, then go somewhere else and don't do business with that company.

provides, the more money they make. The employee has the choice on whether they want to work for that corporation or not.

If you work for a company and you are not appreciated, then go somewhere else and don't do business with that company. As a society, the best way to control irresponsible companies is to not shop there. Another way to control irresponsible companies is to not buy a mutual fund that includes that company in its holdings. As a society, we choose to support or not support the companies we do business with. That's fair.

TAXES

The topic of the economy gets really touchy when it comes to paying everyone's fair share of taxes. It generally comes down to how people without money feel about people with money and vice versa. It has been my experience that some of those without money feel that the rich should pay for the poor. This is usually the same group that has not made good financial choices in their lives. They feel that people who are rich are lucky and didn't have to work for it. Now, I did say *some* of those without money feel this way. I have been on both sides and know that everyone is different. It comes down to how much opportunity and responsibility they have over their lives.

Think about it from a self-responsibility view though. Why should someone who has worked incredibly hard, made good financial choices and took tons of risk, be obligated by law to pay for those who had the same ability but chose not to? That doesn't make any sense to me. This is like a kid who goes trick or treating for six hours and fills up two huge bags of candy and now has to give half of it to the kids that stayed home and watched television all night. Does that make sense? Now don't get me wrong, we should all pay taxes. I enjoy the public library, city streets, highways, mail delivery, police and fire protection, and our military patrolling our borders. Those things need to be paid for. But why should the rich pay more? In many cases, they have worked harder to get what they want.

We recently had a presidential election and one of the candidates was harassed for paying only 14.1% of his income to taxes. This presidential candidate paid $1,935,708 in taxes on $13,696,951 dollars of income.[12] He works hard for his millions and provides numerous jobs. Would it be fair to say that regardless of the percentage he pays, he is paying his fair share of taxes: $1,935,708? Do you pay that much in taxes every year? I don't. Does he get a VIP section at the library or a special HOV lane on the highway? No. Did you know that this same presidential candidate paid over $4,000,000 to charity the same year? What my goal is here is to dispel the myth that the rich are greedy and deserve to pay more taxes. That is ignorance. Some of the greediest people I know happen to be poor. Some of the most giving people I know happen to be rich. You may have had the opposite experience. Being greedy or giving has nothing to do with being rich or poor.

IS MONEY GOOD OR BAD?

As you know I am a self-professed follower of Christ and let me be the first one to tell you that poverty is not what God wants for you. Do you think God and your well-intentioned church wants ten percent of one hundred million dollars or ten percent of fifty bucks? Gandhi was loaded with cash by his supporters and look at all of the good he did. Mother Theresa also had a nice stack of cash donated by the Catholic Church and look how many people she not only helped, but inspired them to help others. The scripture, "The love of money is the root of all evil," has got to be one of the most damaging, misunderstood scriptures in the Bible. The love of *money* is not the root of evil. The love of *greed and power* is the root of all evil, not money. Money is neither good nor evil.

Take out the emotional attachment to the word money and see how off this interpretation is now, "The love of "a tool of exchange" is the root of all evil. The love of "the byproduct of the exchange of services and products" is the root of all evil. The love of "the symbol of achievement, production, the entrepreneurial spirit, freedom, and America" is the root of all evil. Does that make any sense?

I agree that money has the potential to help people do bad things. Money also has the potential to help people do good things. Money itself is not evil. Money is a lot like alcohol. If you give a jerk a large amount of alcohol he is going to be a large jerk. If you give a happy person a great deal of alcohol, they are going to be a great deal happier. If you give a greedy, power-hungry person an excess of money, they are going to be excessively greedy and power hungry. Money is not evil; the person who controls the money has a choice on whether they are going to do good things with it or bad things with it. Money just fuels someone's self-esteem. What actions they take are based on their character and moral code.

DOES MONEY EQUATE TO HAPPINESS?

My family was at our friend and colleague's wedding a few months ago and we gave her and her hubby a nice check as a bonus to spend on their honeymoon. They are both fellow entrepreneurs and we were having a great time. I said to them, "Do you know what my favorite word is? Cha... Do you know what my second favorite word is? Ching!" We all cracked up. Her hubby came back with, "Do you know what is better than money? More money!" Laughs all around.

It is true that money alone does not bring happiness; however, let me be the first to tell you, I have been rich and happy and I have been poor and happy. I would rather be rich and happy. It is good to want the kind of lifestyle that allows you to have a greater impact on the world. It is good to be able to live your dreams. It is good to experience financial and time freedom. It is good to have no debt. It is good to enjoy life free of the discomfort of owing people money. It is good to have the ability to make better choices on where you want your kids to go to school and what part of the world you want to explore, and what quality of food you want to eat. Be open to receiving massive amounts of money.

Most of us know that money is extremely important. When it comes to our happiness, remember, money can buy you a new house, but it cannot buy you a home. Money can buy you a great bed, but it cannot buy you a good night's sleep. It can buy you friends, but it cannot buy you true friendship. It can buy you companionship, but it cannot buy you love. Keep your pursuit about service to the world and you will get your happiness *and* money.

TOP FIVE HABITS OF WEALTH

If you could put your entire wealth plan into five easy habits, and stick to them, and you could have the money, savings, and cash flow of your dreams, would you want to learn them? Me too, again! Make the following five habits part of your daily life and you will eventually have more money than you will ever need. Always have a specific wealth target goal and review the Five-Step Action Jackson every day. When you hit that goal, make a new one.

1. Follow a budget that consists of ten percent to a purpose bigger than yourself, ten percent to your savings, and eighty percent to your fixed and variable expenses.

2. Follow a debt reduction plan. Put an extra fixed amount toward one debt, plus the minimum payment. Once that is paid off,

take the full amount you were paying and put it toward your next debt, plus its minimum payment. Keep up this snowball effect until you are debt free.

3. As soon as your savings reach the equivalent of three months of living expenses, begin to save it in an investment account and follow a wealth accumulation plan which consists of diversified assets that provide long-term growth and cash flow. These can be a combination of businesses, real estate, stocks and bonds, and commodities such as precious metals.

4. As soon as you can, carry five hundred dollars in your pocket at all times and never spend it.

5. Keep a personal financial statement up to date. Know what your assets and liabilities are and track them quarterly.

TOP TEN POVERTY MINDSETS VERSUS WEALTH MINDSETS

Poverty Mindsets	Wealth Mindsets
"I can't afford it."	"How can I afford it?"
"It's too expensive."	"I will be able to buy it soon."
"Rich people are snobs."	"Rich people create jobs and are generous."
"This is all we can do for now."	"Let's do this for now until we can do better."
"I just need to make enough to pay my bills."	"I want to make more than enough."
"Getting money is what my purpose is."	"I want to create value for others and get rich as a result."
"To have money I must work really hard."	"To have money I must work really smart *and* hard."
"I will never be rich."	"How can I create what people need?"
"I will give to the poor when I am not one of them."	"I must give what I want to get now. If I can't give ten percent of ten dollars I am never going to be able to give ten percent of one million."
"We can't."	"How can we?"

Bottom line: Money does not have to be *more important* than other things in your life. Money can be *just as important* as other things in your life. There is no either/or. Money brings you the things and experiences you have always wanted. A healthy relationship with money will affect every area of your life positively.

Elevate

17 Chapter Seventeen:
The Habits of Marriage

*"My most brilliant achievement was my ability to be able
to persuade my wife to marry me."*

-Winston Churchill

*Why relationships? Because if you are alone with no one to
share your life with, you become isolated, which leads to
depression, and it becomes very difficult to focus on
anything else but how sad you are, that's why.* You're destined
for more than that. Is that right or right? Okay, let's start with what
relationships are. Relationships are about being connected. They are
about sharing this experience we call life together. There are obviously
many different personal relationships in your life. You have your
spouse, your kids, your friends, your siblings, your boss, your
coworkers, your acquaintances, etc. Have you ever thought about what
you want in your relationships? Move love? More patience? More
acceptance? More fun?

Let's start with a little trick. Whatever you want more of, you must give
more of. Do you want more love from your spouse? Give them more
love. Do you want to be listened to more? Listen to them more. By the
way, you were born with two ears and one mouth. I'm just saying! Do
you want more respect? Give more respect. Do you need to be more
appreciated? Appreciate more. This is one of those simple rules of life
that aren't necessarily easy, but simple. Give it a shot.

We are going to focus on your spouse relationship and your children
relationship, which hands down, are the two most important
relationships in your life. If you do not have a spouse or kids yet, we
will focus on your future spouse and kids. These relationships are
where you spend most of your life, so make sure you put the time in to
make them incredible. Marriage is a gift. Your children are gifts.

/

LOVE AND MARRIAGE

Fantastic marriages require fantastic individuals. If you have it together individually, you will have it together as a couple. My definition of a fabulous marriage is one that is based on unconditional love and commitment, communication, and total acceptance of one another with a shared purpose and vision. I know this is a big aspiration to shoot for, but regardless of where your marriage is now, shoot for it to always get better.

If you are not married yet, do you know what you want in a spouse? Do you know what questions to ask? When you choose a spouse, you are choosing someone to spend the rest of your life with. This person becomes a part of you, and together you will share your life's missions. Let's start from the beginning. In the beginning, there was love....and it was good...

CHOOSING A SPOUSE

I'm sure you have heard that opposites attract. This is true in many love relationships with regards to strengths and weaknesses but not so much in values. In a previous chapter, we talked about different personality types. Many times, not all times, but many times, couples share the opposite personality traits in order to balance out the relationship. This is a good thing because as the two of you become one, you can act as a more complete functional unit, "you complete me," right? If you are super formal, you may attract someone who is informal. If you are super dominant, you may attract someone who is easy going. This certainly isn't required for choosing a spouse; however, it is fun to watch when you meet couples. Sometimes, both in the relationship are very similar in personality traits, and that works fine, too. These couples tend be very balanced at giving each other control when necessary.

Remember, a fabulous marriage is based on unconditional love and commitment, communication, and total acceptance of one another with a shared purpose and vision.

If you are on the hunt for the love of your life, choose wisely. Read the questions below so you can prescreen your potential spouse. If you are in a relationship, and marriage is being considered, take the time to ask them some questions to make sure you know what you are getting yourself into.

/

When I first was considering asking my beautiful wife to marry me, we went out for ice cream, and I totally drilled her with questions. She thought I was a little militant about it, but I needed to make sure my head was lining up with my heart. It was the best choice I ever made. Remember, a fabulous marriage is based on unconditional love and commitment, communication, and total acceptance of one another with a shared purpose and vision.

When you are in love and feeling the "feelings" all of the time, you will know when things are getting "serious." Asking these serious potential deal breaker questions may be the last thing you feel like doing. With the divorce rate over fifty percent, it is pretty clear that not lining up your head *with* your heart does not work for most.

When it comes to new relationships, do you both know that what you see right now is what you get? This is similar for career interviews, too. How they are showing up to you in the first two days is the best presentation of themselves that they have. If you are picking up too many red flags during this initial process, then it's time to do the moonwalk, back up and head out. Typically, the best you are ever going to have is what is in front of you right now. The point is, your future spouse may or may not *ever* change, so certainly be totally accepting of who they are and what they stand for right here, right now. We can all use improvement, but remember, you cannot change someone unless they are willing and coachable.

If you are already married, then these can be good questions to work through and strengthen your relationship. As a side note, I do not believe that getting a woman pregnant is reason for marriage. If that has happened, accept the fact that you both messed up big time and it's time to be responsible and move forward. For the men out there, if you do not want to get married to each other, then BE A MAN and support her and your future child. Not getting married does not mean you are not going to be a dad. Be that kid's dad, man. Break the cycle of children being raised without fathers. It starts with you! Buck up and be there from the start for your future little buckaroo.

TWENTY QUESTIONS TO ASK YOURSELF REGARDING YOUR RELATIONSHIP WITH A POTENTIAL SPOUSE BEFORE CONSIDERING MARRIAGE:

1. Do your personalities complement each other? Do they bring out the best personality in you? Take an online personality test together one night for fun. This will really start the process of getting to know who you are considering marrying and what you are getting yourself into.

2. Do you still have a lot of fun together? Do you love each other's company?

3. Do you share common interests or hobbies?

4. Do you both know what you love about the other?

5. Do you both have strong sexual chemistry toward each other?

6. Do you both know each other's deal breaker rules for relationships?

7. Have you both read this book? Seriously. Make sure that you are considering marrying someone who knows who they are, why they are here, and what they want.

8. Have you gotten to know their family? Do they get along with their mom and dad? How well do they treat their parents?

9. Do you know their closest friends? What do they like to do with their friends?

10. How well do you both communicate or deal with stress in the relationship? Does that need to be worked on, or are you both good there?

11. Why did their past relationships end? What happened? What did they learn from them?

12. What are the red flags that you have noticed in your head but have ignored up to this point? Do those need to be discussed?

13. What does marriage mean to them? What do they believe about marriage?

14. What roles would you both have in the marriage? Who does what?

15. Do they like kids? Do they want children? How many? How do they want their future kids raised? What does family mean to them?

16. Do you line up spiritually? Do they have good character and moral code? Would you feel comfortable having them be the example for your future children?

17. Do you share the same lifestyle health habits? Are you on the same page on how to stay healthy? Do you both have the same health philosophy?

18. What do they do for income? Are you going to be satisfied financially with their current status as well as their potential? What is their relationship with money?

19. What is important to them and what is their life mission? Are you both on the same page with loving God, being your best, and helping others?

20. Where do they see the two of you in five years, ten years, twenty years?

Okay, how does your potential mate stand up or how does your spouse stand up? These are some deep questions. You need to decide which ones are your deal breakers and which ones you can live with. These twenty questions are the fundamentals. If you have ever been divorced, after reading these questions, is it pretty clear why the marriage didn't work? If this is you, you deserve a loving relationship regardless of what happened, so go get it again!

MARRIAGE A LITTLE ROCKY?

Now, with all that being said, know from the beginning that marriage is not always bliss. Whenever you meet a couple who has a great marriage, it is because they know how to ride through the ups and downs. Marriage is about commitment and communication. As long as each other's needs are being met, you really can have a life-long happy marriage. I used to think that when I met a couple that had a great marriage, it is because they never fight...ha! Not true. They do argue, they do take space from each other, and they do lose their cool with each other at times. With all of that being said, they also know that their commitment is more important than how they feel at the time. They give each other space when needed. They argue respectfully most of the time and they communicate effectively. If you and your spouse are going through a rocky time right now, really spend some time on the next two sections. You both are worth it.

I said before that fantastic marriages are made up between two fantastic individuals. That means that you each live by the principles in this book, or similar principles that keep you happy. Look, if you are not happy, your spouse will not be happy. You need to be happy first, and then you can bring your light into the marriage. Your spouse is not there to be the sole source of your happiness! You must be happy first and then the spouse magnifies that and makes your happiness even stronger. Now I hope you know that just because you live by the principles of this book doesn't mean every day is going to be a fantastic day for you or your marriage. These principles take a lifetime to get down. Even as the author, I think I have made it clear that I individually am a work in progress, my fantastic marriage is a work in progress, just like you, just like him, just like her, just like all of us.

> Your spouse is not there to be the sole source of your happiness!

If you have neglected your marriage so far to the point of considering divorce, take a minute to do a self-analysis. Number one, if you both are willing to give your marriage a fighting chance then move forward with these considerations. I repeat, if you both are willing to give it a shot then commit to giving it a shot. Consider the following point of view. You are bringing you into your current marriage. If you have failed to give your marriage the same attention you give your career, health, and any other key area in your life, then it is not acceptable as a self-responsible individual to throw in the towel and give up. If you got divorced, you would just bring your same self into the next marriage.

Everything that you do not like about your spouse can be addressed, confronted, changed or accepted if you both are willing to. If you think it would be better on the other side of the fence with someone else, then that new person may be better at the things you are seeking or may be better at fulfilling the needs you are missing, but they will not be as good as the things your current spouse is already doing that you don't realize you love so much. The new marriage will just bring new issues to work on. The key is knowing that improvement in the relationship with yourself and the relationship with your spouse is constant and never ending. Marriage is not about not having any issues. Marriage is about accepting each other completely. There is not a perfect spouse folks, just ask my wife. There is no such thing as a perfect human being!

Look, take an honest assessment of *yourself*. Would you be married to you? Are you at a level ten in all areas of your life? Do you communicate one hundred percent effectively? Are you completely spiritually at peace? Do you have an incredible body and consider yourself a sexy beast? Are you the parent of the year? Do you never lose your temper? Are you loaded with tons of cash and free time? If you do have *all* of these, let me know the name of your book. I would love to read it.

Married couples who get divorced most always end up getting remarried, and studies show the divorce rate to be much higher on marriages after their first.[13] Divorce is giving up on *your* self-growth. If you are reading this book, you are not someone who is like most people. You have the intellectual knowledge to not make the same decisions that over half of married couples do, divorce. You are smarter, better at this, and playing the game of life at a higher level than that.

Be honest with your spouse and let them know your needs are not being met. Ask them what needs are not being met for them. Commit to each other's needs again. Accept what you need to finally accept about the other, and get into mutual agreement on your needs. Commit to making it work.

If you think that being single for the rest of your life is the way to go, well, I would encourage you to talk to someone who has been single for over a year. Being single long term works for a very small group of people. The life of no responsibility, empty sex, and no one to answer to, is not your answer. There is a reason rock stars and movie stars get married, folks. Life is meant to be experienced with a partner. Create the "remember when" with your spouse.

Of course, the choice is ultimately yours, and of course, there are rule breakers for absolute divorce; however, if divorce is being considered, at least sit down and read this book together. Stay away from people who believe that marriage is terrible. Get around people who know every marriage has two individuals that are works in progress. Get on the same team and be friends along the path. If you are not happy in your marriage, it is because a need is not being met. When you don't feel like communicating, what do you need to do? Communicate.

MARRIAGE BEST PRACTICES

If you have decided that you want a better marriage, you are reading the right book. Marriages will always have ups and downs; it is part of the game. It does take work and it is not always easy. The following list is my top ten for keeping myself and my wife fulfilled in *our* marriage. This list is for the married men out there. If you want an awesome marriage, here is your action plan:

1. Appreciate her every day. I'm not kidding. Tell her how special she is to you and why, every day. I know fellas, just trust me on

this one. Sorry ladies, we need to be told to do this stuff. If you want a great marriage, just roll with this.

2. Make sure you know what makes her feel loved and schedule it in a variety of ways every week. Yes, schedule it. If you don't know, ask her. If she doesn't know, then take the Five Love Languages Quiz online and find out.

3. Be clear on each other's needs. What does she need on a regular basis to feel like she is in a solid, committed relationship? Make sure you both are clear on your roles in the marriage. I do this and you do this kinda thing.

4. Remain clear about each other's rules. "What are your deal breaker rules and what can we come together on mutual agreement with? Okay, here are mine. Are we both in agreement on each other's rules? Are we both in agreement on the consequences if these are broken?" I know this sounds very business-like, but marriage needs rules. Two people on the same team will only work if both of them know what the rules are.

5. Keep the sexual chemistry going. This is touchy, but I want the best for you both. Are you both still in the same shape you were in when you got married? Hubby, are you carrying around a big beer gut now and wonder why you are not sexually stimulated by your wife? Work on getting sexy yourself, Fabio, and then see how sexy you find your wife. Both hubby and wifey need to take continued care of their health. It is not fair not to. Keep it spicy folks. Get your sexy on.

6. Schedule a date night every week. Go enjoy a night out together without the kids weekly. This is the time to not only have fun but to ask each other, "On a scale of one to ten, how would you rate our marriage this week? Okay, what can I work on this week specifically to bring it back to a ten?"

7. There can be no concealments with your wife. None. If you can't talk to your wife with pure vulnerability then that is a big challenge to work on. Tell your wife everything. Look, if you have some concealments that you don't think you could ever talk to her about, do me a favor and re-read the Forgiveness of Self and Others chapter. Get some help if you have to. I care about you too much as a fellow human being to not let your soul die inside because you think you could never tell her the truth. Marriage *is* sacred. If you are sincerely sorry and you discuss it openly with her, and she is not willing to forgive you, then, brother, it may not work out. That is the risk you must take to

be happy. Nothing is worth you losing your soul over by not revealing concealments. Remember, marriage is total acceptance of one another.

8. Have a common unified purpose. What can you both work toward that is bigger than each other or your marriage? This could be a spiritual purpose. It could be a helping mankind purpose. Whatever is most important to you that is a cause bigger than yourself, unite with your wife on it, and make that purpose happen together.

9. Your wife needs to know you are committed no matter what. I know they like to push us away sometimes, but just make sure she knows that you love her unconditionally and will be right there when she is ready. If you ever need space, make sure she knows you love her but need to be alone and will be back.

10. Make sure you both know that you are on the same team. You can never "win" an argument with your wife. Think about that. You win, she feels terrible, but hey, you won. That doesn't work. Don't argue, communicate. It is too destructive to argue. It is better to step away if it comes down to useless nonproductive arguing. Never explain away her feelings.

TEN MARRIAGE COMMUNICATION GEMS

The following are a few relationship communication gems I have picked up over the years. They can apply to any relationship you have and are particularly helpful with your love relationship.

1. I mentioned earlier that what you don't respect, you lose. This is a reality big time when it comes to relationships. Have you ever been talking to your spouse and your mind is completely somewhere else? Of course you have. I have for sure. Guys, listen to this one for our gals out there. The key to being present with your wife when your mind starts to wander is to mentally remind yourself of all the reasons you appreciate her. This brings you right back to focusing on what you need to be focusing on, your beautiful wife.

2. Always be interested in what your spouse has to say. Focus on being *interested*, not *interesting* all of the time. People want to talk about themselves and your spouse is no different.

3. When you need something from your spouse, talk in their values. Find out what they want and communicate in a way that helps them get what they want. For example, "Honey, I would

like to go fishing with my friends this Saturday. I will call up the babysitter and make sure she is available to watch the kids so you can have some downtime and go out with your friends if you would like." Hey, marriage is always about win/win.

4. When communicating with your spouse, never be assumptive. Don't assume you know where they are coming from and then avoid confrontation. If you want to avoid some drama in your marriage, if you feel upset, have the courage to confront them and find out where they are coming from.

5. Do you use sarcasm in your relationships? Did you know that sarcasm is always, always perceived as a threat? For example, you forget to take out the trash and your spouse says, "Honey, *thanks a lot for taking out the trash,* just kidding!" That comment will always come back to bite the person who says it. Maybe not today, but it's coming.

6. Never criticize your spouse. Remember we are all works in progress. Be super slow to criticize and quick to appreciate. Appreciate your spouse, appreciate your spouse, appreciate your spouse. Did I say appreciate your spouse earlier?

7. If your spouse is upset with you and you have no idea why, ask to find out what's going on. If you still have no idea why and something is just off with them, it is usually because they have done something against *you* that you are not aware of and they are not happy or proud about it. Ask them about it with no judgment until it comes out because this kind of fester can destroy the relationship. Now that is some Jedi mind magic.

8. When needing to confront your spouse, don't say, "We need to talk." That always conjures up fear. Instead say, "I need your help. I need to clarify a couple of things." Big difference right? Right!

9. If you ever do not feel like communicating, it is time to communicate. If it looks like an argument is about to happen, nip it in the bud and ask her lovingly, "What do you want?" This is the fastest way to end the argument or prevent it.

10. Compliment her in front of others and always help her shine. Brag on her! Make her feel like the bomb with sincere compliments on who she is, what she did, and how awesome you think she is!

If you could put your entire marriage plan into five easy habits, and you could have the love life of your dreams if you stuck to them, would you want to learn them? Me too, again and again! Make the following five habits part of your daily life and you will eventually have more love from your spouse than you will ever need. Always have a specific marriage target goal and review the Five-Step Action Jackson every day. When you hit that goal, make a new one.

TOP FIVE HABITS OF MARRIAGE

1. Take action on what makes your spouse feel loved weekly.

2. Have a date night once a week.

3. Reflect weekly on what is going well and what can be improved.

4. Keep the sex life sexy.

5. Ask each other daily if there is anything that they need help with.

Bottom line: Make the best choice with the tools you have when choosing a spouse. Continue to follow best practices of marriage if you want to spend your life happy. Your marriage will affect every area of your life. Make it a great one.

Elevate

18 Chapter Eighteen:
The Habits of Parenting

"It is easier to build strong children than to repair broken men."

-Frederick Douglass

I'm assuming if you have kids, you want them to be incredible. If you do have kids or want kids, you will love what you are about to read. Kids are such a gift to us, aren't they? Parenting is a privilege, and in my opinion, a trusted gift from God. Children are one of the greatest joys in life. Our job as parents is to give them the tools they need to succeed in life. Now remember, this goes without being said, you are the example! You must live the *Elevate* life if you want your kids to live the *Elevate* life.

> *"Do as I say, not as I do, does not work"*

Do as I say, not as I do, does not work. If you smoke, your kids will be open to smoking, regardless of what excuse you give them. You are their hero! If you yell at your spouse, your kids will be open to yelling at their future spouse. If you talk about money in a poverty mindset way your kids will talk about money in a poverty mindset way. Parenting is your opportunity to break any generational curses and give your kids the *Elevate* mindset. If you want more for your kids than you have for yourself, you have the power to make that happen.

Don't be the parent that says, "This is the way I am because this is the way my parents were, and this is the way I am going to allow you to be for your life and your future kid's lives." Sounds crazy, right? Break the cycle! I know you would have never gotten this far in the book if you were not the kind of person that has the courage to see where your parenting falls short. If it is time for a U-turn, then crank the wheel now. We are all holding on! We are talking about not only their future, but yours, and mine, and your neighbors! I'm done with kids bringing shotguns to school! You?

My guess is if you are a parent, it is pretty safe to say that one of the things you want is for them to develop into a happy, healthy, *elevated* mindset adult. I have put together a few lists that my wife and I practice. Our boys are fantastic and we are very proud of them. Our goal is to make sure we develop them to become highly functioning people for as long as we have them under our influence. If we do it right, my hope is that our mentorship will be forever in some way.

Can you imagine if you had two loving parents that took the time to invest in you the way you are going to begin to invest in your kids? Yeah! Think how long it took you to learn what this book is all about. Can you imagine how much farther you would be ahead if it didn't take you thirty years to learn to eat right and exercise, for example? Can you imagine if you were trained as a child to invest ten percent of your money every week? Parenting is a blessing, folks.

Before we dive into the lessons I have learned and want to share with you, I must come clean and let you know that both of my boys have not yet reached ten years old. I firmly believe that one should only take advice from those they want to be like. My wife and I have not been involved in the parenting process to its completion yet. I will tell you that we get compliments on our kids all of the time, though. It is my belief that we are doing a great job; however, we are still midrace.

THIRTEEN HABITS TO DEVELOP YOUR KIDS THE ELEVATE WAY

How we communicate with our children shows them how to be effective and fully functioning now and in their adulthood. The following are the top ways you can communicate with your children to ensure that they develop the skills to get what they want as they get older. I have attempted to put them in order of use based on their age.

1. Speak positive affirmations into their lives every night at bedtime.

   Example: You say, "I believe in you! You are destined for greatness! You can do anything you set your mind to! You are a champ, you know that, Tiger?" You are setting them up for a positive self-esteem and an "I can do it" attitude!

2. Don't tell them no, tell them to stop.

   Example: Your child pulls on the cat's tail. Instead of saying, "No! No! No!" say, "STOP!" This trains their mind that it is okay to take risks when they want to. Instead of their minds being programmed to always say no when they want to take a risk, their minds will become programmed to stop instead and think about what they are about to do and proceed if they would like to.

3. Address the behavior not the child.

   Example: Your child throws a toy across the room. You say, "Johnny, we don't throw toys across the room. That is not acceptable behavior." We don't say, "Johnny you are a bad boy for throwing the toy across the room."

4. Teach them manners—"excuse me," "please," and "thank you."

   Example: Your child interrupts you midsentence while you are talking to another adult. You say to your child, "Wait until there is a break in the conversation and say excuse me." Whenever the opportunity arises, always have them repeat out loud "please" and "thank you." Did you know that studies show that people who say please and thank you are more trusted?

5. Make them ask for what they want and don't let them say they can't do something.

   Example: Your child says, "I'm thirsty!" You say, "Okay, tell me what you want." They say, "I want a glass of water." Example: Your child says, "I can't reach the water glass." You say, "Don't tell me what you can't do, tell me what you need."

6. Tell them what to do, not what not to do.

   Example: If your child is carrying a large glass of almond milk, don't say, "Don't drop that glass." Do say, "Hold on to that glass, tightly." This trains their minds to think in a positive way and to think about what they *want* and not what they *don't want*.

7. Don't dismiss what they say as not being important.

   Example: Your child says, "Mommy, the sun is up right now!" You say, "That is right, angel! You are so smart!" Do not say, "Duh, it comes up every morning, silly!" When we teach our children that what they have to say is important, and we validate that, it gives them the confidence to speak up when they need to.

8. Avoid use of the words: try, but, should, could, and maybe.

   Examples: Try—Your child says, "I'll try to pick up my room." You say, "Do you mean you are going to pick up your room?" Do or do not. Do not try. Would/But—Your child says, "I would pick up my room but I want to do my homework first." You say, "Do you mean, you *will* pick up your room *and* you want to do your homework first?" Should/Could—Your child says, "I should pick up my room today. I could pick up my room today." You say, "Do you mean, I must pick up my room today; I can pick up my room today?"

9. When your kids ask you for something, see if they can figure it out themselves first.

   Example: Your child says, "What is the capital of Colorado?" You say, "Hmmm, how would you get the answer to that? Let's look it up online together and see if you can figure it out on your own." Guide them to the source of the answer instead of just giving it to them. Train them to be solutions people.

10. Let them work out sibling fights on their own.

    Example: They say, "Mommy, Billy hit me!" You say, "Talk it out together and then let me know what the solution is." If they are unable to do that, give them suggestions and have them come back when they have worked it out. If they refuse to work it out, have them go in their rooms until they do.

11. It's not did you win, it's did you do your best?

    Example: Your child comes home from her volleyball game. You say, "Did you do your best?" You do not say, "Did you win? Did you win?" If we are only happy if they win, it teaches them that you give them love only when they achieve something, instead of loving them because they are a human being. Hello, fellow Type A's.

12. Teach them to use the word "I" not "you."

    Example: The child is talking about themselves and says, "You know when you get pushed around and you get really mad?" You say, "Do you mean to say, you know when I get pushed around and I get really mad?" Many of us explain how we feel using the word "you" instead of "I" when we are talking about ourselves. This allows them to not be responsible for how they feel. This teaches them that everyone experiences and feels the same way about life as they do, and they don't.

13. Don't let them ask for money.

    Example: Your child says, "Dad, can I have some money?" You say, "Do you mean how can you earn some money?" Money is earned and kids learn the value early. When they know they need to earn their own money to get the things and experiences they want, they become resourceful and very creative.

If you could put your entire parenting plan into five easy habits that if you stuck to, you would have the kids of your dreams, would you want to learn them? Me too, again and again and again! Make the following five habits part of your daily life and you will eventually have the best children on the planet! Always have a specific parenting target goal and review the Five-Step Action Jackson every day. When you hit that goal, make a new one.

TOP FIVE HABITS OF PARENTING

1. Hug and love them every day.

2. Spend individual time with them weekly doing something they enjoy.

3. Schedule and teach them weekly about the principles in this book.

4. Discipline their behavior and not them as a person.

5. Always have them in an extracurricular activity so they can discover what their passions are.

Bottom line: Give your kids the tools to grow into leaders that can be the change to see the change. One of the most rewarding relationships you will ever have is the one with your children. Be the incredible parent that is raising children intentionally.

Chapter Nineteen:
Rituals and Reflection

"I love those who can smile in trouble, who can gather strength from distress, and grow brave by reflection. 'Tis the business of little minds to shrink, but they whose heart is firm, and whose conscience approves their conduct, will pursue their principles unto death."

-Leonardo da Vinci

Are you a driver or producer? Do you need to slow down sometimes, okay, a lot of times? Remember when heart attacks were only for old people? Not anymore. People in their thirties and forties have them every day. Why is it that some of our personality types race through life, but we don't want to get to the end? Setting up rituals and reflections will keep us in the game of creating the life we want; a life that has the winning combination of getting what we want *and* having fun in the process.

DAILY RITUALS

Every successful leader I know has a morning ritual. It's a morning focus time, and it is your daily creation plan. This is a fundamental to creating the life you want. It is an absolute necessity to being fulfilled and not just accomplished. I want to share with you what my daily ritual is. Take the parts you like, discard the parts you don't, and create your own. This is what I do upon rising. It works for me!

1. Attitude—Upon rising, I get out of bed, stretch and say something like this to myself, "Today is going to be a beautiful day!"

2. Read—I read for about five minutes. This is usually Success Magazine or a current inspirational book I am reading.

3. Exercise—I go for a run or lift weights. I am a fan of the twenty minute workout club!

4. Audio—On my drive to work, I feed my mind with positive audios.

5. Spiritual—I am usually the first person to get to our office. Outside my office window is a beautiful view of downtown skyscrapers and the mountains. It is very inspirational to me. I sit at my desk, tell God everything I am grateful for, and then set my timer for three minutes of silence. I quiet my mind and still my thoughts. I meditate and visualize Christ's love and shining white light coming from His chest in the sky directly into my chest as I breathe deeply in and out. When my timer goes off, I ask God for guidance in my life. And yes, I usually get at least one specific thing to work on for the day to pop into my head.

6. Be-Do-Have—I get out my Be-Do-Have sheet that I created around the four most important areas of my life. I affirm my life purpose, my priorities, and my core values. I then go through my four most important categories: God, Health, Family, and Wealth. For each category I read what kind of person I need to be to achieve what I want in each area. I then read what I must do daily to achieve what I want in each area. I then read what I want to have in each area. Lastly, I read *why* I want, what I want to achieve, in each area.

7. Affirm and Visualize—I then say out loud a few affirmations and quotes that inspire me. After that, I conclude my morning focus time by closing my eyes and visualizing what I want in each area of my life.

From there it's business time! I review the top three objectives for the day, write down what I need to do that day to achieve them, and then I check messages, email, and my calendar. I hit up my action folder and make it happen! I set my alarm to go off at 11:00 and 3:00 to check my messages and email again, and to take three deep breaths filled with gratitude, and to watch a funny two-minute video online. On the way home, I listen to inspirational audios again, and once I get home, I switch gears from work to family and do my best to become the best husband and daddy in the world! (echo for effect) World... world...world....

This sounds like a lot as I write it out, but it is habit now and doesn't take much mental effort or time effort. Your rituals will make your life easy. Aren't you ready to stop battling your bed? Battling your snooze button? Battling your career? Battling your stress? Set up the rituals to get what you want. What kind of rituals do you have? Are they getting you closer to getting what you want?

WEEKLY REFLECTION

Once a week, make an appointment with yourself with a cup of coffee or tea. Sit down and ask yourself the following questions:

1. On a scale of one to ten, how happy am I this week?

2. On a scale of one to ten, how would I rank my health, wealth, and relationships?

3. Do I need to address anything and make any decisions?

4. Am I achieving what I have set out to accomplish?

5. Am I continually committed to the direction I am headed?

If you are on track, then keep it going; if you are not, then recognize it. Recognize where you are off; stop doing whatever you are doing that is taking you off track; decide what corrections are needed to get you back on track; commit to it; and do it! This is literally your results guidance system. You are looking at your results, making corrections as you go, and moving forward.

If you have a lot of unanswered maybes in your life, it will affect you in more ways than you know.

This weekly appointment with yourself will become the most important appointment you have when going after what you want. If you have a lot of unanswered "maybes" in your life, it will affect you in more ways than you know. People who have too many "maybes" in their life respond slower in communication and in their thought process. They have a long list of unfinished projects in their life and have a hard time making decisions. Be the person that clears up any "maybes" at a minimum of once a week. Be the person that loves themselves enough to get back on track and make corrections as you go.

THE GUT CHECK

This reflection tool is one that is especially helpful if you are stuck in a rut. If you have numerous difficulties in your life and things just aren't going the way you want it to, there is a reason. That reason is usually easier for other people to see who are like-minded and on the same path than it is for us to see ourselves. If you find yourself spinning your wheels, ask a trusted friend or mentor the following Gut Check questions.

1. How do I show up to you?

2. What are my strengths?

3. What are my areas that need improvement?

4. Do you see any areas in my life where I am sabotaging myself?

5. What do you see that I should start or stop doing to help me achieve what I want?

These questions need to be asked to someone who you trust and have a very authentic relationship with. These questions are the ones you ask to those who are on your side, your balcony people, your friends along the path. Even if you are not stuck, ask someone the Gut Check questions anyway to make sure you are not missing anything. You might be surprised on how your answers and their answers may be different.

> **Bottom line:** Commit to starting your day off with the power of your morning ritual! Take time to reflect on your vision and make sure you have the right people around you that will help guide you back when needed.

Part Five

The *Elevate* Practicals
The Pillars in Action

Elevate

Chapter Twenty: Conclusion

"The great end of life is not knowledge, but action."

-Francis Bacon

Daht, daht, daaaaaa! Congratulations on making it to the end of Elevate! Of course you know this is just the beginning. As I stated in the introduction, I truly feel that the book you have just read will set you on a path that will result in everything you want and desire.

This book is your *Ultimate Life Success Formula* to achieve what you want. It is your formula for ultimate happiness and fulfillment. You elevated your foundational self; you discovered who you are and why you are here. You learned the *Elevate* mindset and you determined what you want. You also discovered the habits that will help you get what you want.

THE ULTIMATE LIFE SUCCESS FORMULA:

1. Elevate your foundational self

2. Know who you are and why you are here

3. Implement the *Elevate* Mindset

4. Determine what you want

5. Develop the habits to achieve what you want

Now it is time for action. This final section is the one that brings it all together for you! This is the section that takes everything you have learned intellectually and turns it into results! I urge, ask, plead, beseech, appeal, beg, and any other synonym I can look up, DO THESE PRACTICALS! They will cement what you have learned deep into your nervous system so that you will truly be a living example of *Elevate*! I will be the first one to admit, some of these practicals are going to take an extreme amount of courage. You may want to get a friend and go through the practicals together. No matter what, do each and every one of them in order. I promise you there is a method to the madness, the madness, I tell you!

Following the Adult Practicals are the Kid Practicals. If you have children, the Kid Practicals will set your kids up for success!

In the introduction I mentioned our website, www.Elevate Book.com/Bonus. Take the free Elevate Score at www.Elevate Book.com/Bonus and see where you rank before you perform these practicals, if you haven't done so already. While you're there, get your free Elevate Affirmations poster. If you want to experience more Elevate in person, check out our next upcoming Elevate Experience Event on our site. I hope to meet you there soon!

In summary, we dove deep into your life! You are now on the path again to success. Stay on it. When you are happy, people around you are happy. When you are a fully functioning human being, tackling life's challenges and caring for each other at the same time, others will want the same for their life. When you have it all together and are an example of what success looks like, people will want what you have. You are going to face challenges. There will be ups and downs. Pick this book back up. Read the chapter you know you need to read and move forward again. Continue to become more to have more. Continue to let your light shine no matter how dim it gets at times. The world needs you.

> *When you are a fully functioning human being, tackling life's challenges and caring for each other at the same time, others will want the same for their life.*

The purpose of this book is bigger than you and I. The purpose is to start a movement by being *the change* so we can *see the change*. Our country is facing a huge challenge. Many of us are so busy trying to just survive life that we are rarely focused on anything else. So many of us are looking for fast, easy solutions to solve our problems and our unhappiness. I believe this book can help stop that cycle. This book can help stop the insanity that is on the news every night.

As I said in the introduction, no more school shootings, folks. Many solutions have been discussed as far as locking down our schools and adding surveillance systems and armed security. This may help to an extent; however, the fundamental solution is to start with ourselves. Remember the Gandhi quote, "You must be the change you wish to see in the world."

If you have children or want children in the future, remember, if you are happy, your kids are happy. If you have love for yourself, you have love for your children. Kids who feel loved do not bring guns into schools. Be the person that is the example to others and especially to your children. Teach them what love is. Teach them what a strong character looks like. Teach them what is right and wrong. Teach them to forgive themselves and others and to totally accept themselves just the way they are. Teach them to believe in themselves. Get them on the right path. Help them discover their strengths and gifts. Teach them their purpose. Develop them as responsible human beings that have a great attitude.

We can do this. You can do this. It starts with you. I believe in you...

ELEVATE PRACTICALS—ADULT

PART ONE: THE ELEVATE SELF—YOUR BEGINNING TO GREATNESS

CHAPTER ONE: LOVE

Fundamental One: Love Your Creator

Practical: Go outside and stretch your arms out wide and look up toward the sky and shout to the hilltops, "I love my creator!" Hold your pose for ten seconds and feel your love shoot to the sky.

Fundamental Two: Love Yourself

Practical: Give yourself a huge hug and say to yourself, "I love you just the way you are! I love everything about you! I love you!" Keep the embrace as long as you feel love coming from you to you!

Fundamental Three: Love People

Practical: Get a friend and go to the store and buy five flowers each. Walk up to five strangers that you feel drawn to and give them a flower and say, "You matter, and I love you as a person." Ask them if you can give them a hug. If they say yes, then do it. If they don't, you have planted a seed and your gesture will grow in their life.

CHAPTER TWO: CHARACTER

Fundamental Four: The Big Six: Honesty, Respect, Loyalty, Faith, Courage, and Love

Practical: Invite a friend out for coffee or tea and list out the Big Six on a sheet of paper and give yourself a ranking of one to ten. Put them in order of lowest to highest. Start with the lowest and write down at least one way you can strengthen each character trait that needs strengthening. Put your notes on a small notecard and carry it with you for a week. Share with your friend what experiences you had for the week and how you consciously were put to the test and how well you did. At the end of the week, rank them again and continue the process until you are happy with the score you are giving yourself.

CHAPTER THREE: MORAL CODE

Fundamental Five: The Bad Six: Lie, Cheat, Steal, Destroy, Mentally Harm, or Physically Abuse.

Practical: Ask yourself if you are doing any of the Bad Six. If they are happening regularly, decide to stop doing them. Admit to yourself today that you are a work in progress and you have officially committed to stopping the Bad Six. Ask for help if you need it, but commit to ending the self-destruction you are creating. If you are not doing these regularly, commit to these fundamental moral codes in all interactions with others. Tell the next person you see that you are committing to living at your highest potential and say, "I am a person that avoids The Bad Six. I do not: lie, cheat, steal, destroy, mentally harm, or physically abuse others. I love myself and people. I commit to treating people the way I want to be treated."

Fundamental Six: Get Clear on Your Ethics in Each Category

Practical: Decide for yourself where you stand on: euthanasia, capital punishment, homosexuality, gambling, lust and envy, abortion, pride, premarital sex, animal abuse, recreational drugs and alcohol, prescription drugs, environment, gun control, welfare and health care. Ask a good friend to do the same and respectfully discuss how each of you feel and stand on each ethical issue. Ask each other if you can both agree on the Bad Six and respect each other's points of view on the others. The key to this practical is not to be right. The key is to determine where you stand on these issues at this point in your life.

CHAPTER FOUR: FORGIVENESS OF SELF AND OTHERS

Fundamental Seven: Forgive Yourself

Practical: Review the six steps in the Forgiveness of Self section and perform them if you need to. Really spend some time determining if you have performed something in your past that you need to let go of now. One of the steps includes making it right if you still have the opportunity to. Do this step if it is an option.

Fundamental Eight: Forgive Others

Practical: Review the eight steps in the Forgiving Others section. If you have someone you are not forgiving, then follow the formula. Spend some extra time on finding out how the action you need to forgive has served you in some way for the positive.

Practical: Have a friend slap you in the face at medium force. You want to feel it. Don't get yourself knocked out, but feel it. Have them go for the other cheek, but this time, defend yourself and block it. Grab the person's arm and say to them, "Hurt people, hurt people. I love you." Discuss the emotions you felt with this exercise with your friend. Now it is your turn to slap them and feel how it feels on the other side.

CHAPTER FIVE: SELF-ACCEPTANCE AND SEEKING APPROVAL

Fundamental Nine: Accept Yourself

Practical: Grab a friend and make a list of everything you do not like about your appearance or used to not like until you accepted it. Share the list with your friend and vice versa. Read the Authenticity section together and see if you can admit to yourself that everyone has physical appearance issues that they need to accept about themselves. Tell your friend, "I accept this, this, and this about myself. This is who I am, and I love it!" Now dare each other to go up to a stranger and say it again. I dare ya!

Practical: Walk down the street and make eye contact, smile and say hello to at least ten people in two minutes.

Practical: Make a large sign that says, I LOVE MYSELF! HONK! Go to a busy street corner and hold it up above your head. Don't wear any sunglasses and smile big. Stay in that activity until you get at least three honks.

Practical: Make another large sign that says, I DO NOT NEED YOUR APPROVAL TO BE HAPPY. Hang this one around your neck and walk through an outdoor mall from one end to the other.

PART TWO: THE ELEVATE PURPOSE—WHO ARE YOU?

CHAPTER SIX: BELIEVE IN YOURSELF

Fundamental Ten: I Believe in Me

Practical: Make a list of fifty things you have accomplished and are proud of in your life. Start as early as you can remember and don't stop until you have fifty. Pick your top five and share them with someone you love.

Practical: Dig deep and ask yourself if what you say, think, and do is consistent. Reveal any inconsistencies and move in the right direction to make them right. Write, What I Say, Think, and Do is Consistent! on a Post-it note and place it somewhere you are going to see it every day.

Practical: Take a friend to a restaurant and stand up and say, "I believe in myself!" Sit back down and enjoy your meal.

Practical: Go somewhere outside where there are crowds of people. Place a large sign beside you that reads, I BELIEVE IN MYSELF! Stand while holding a hat faced upward and shout, "I believe that someone will put money in my hat!" Say this over and over until someone puts money in your hat. Get super convicted on this one and do not stop until you have convinced someone by your conviction that you truly do believe in yourself! Cha Ching!

CHAPTER SEVEN: RECOGNIZING YOUR STRENGTHS AND PRIORITIES

Fundamental Eleven: Core Values

Practical: List out your top five to seven core values that strongly resonate with you. Ask yourself if you died tomorrow, what core values would you like people to say you represented. Make this list on a sheet of paper and begin to review it every day. Know that once you decide to become your core values you will have your core values. After you write down your core values, write another page, titled, Who Am I?

Fundamental Twelve: Key Areas of Life: God, Health, Family, Wealth

Practical: On a sheet of paper, write on the top, Key Areas of Life. List out your fundamental beliefs in each of these categories. Choose no more than five sentences to describe how you think about each of these areas. Begin to review these every day along with your core values. They may change, and if they do, update your sheet and adopt your new beliefs in each area.

Fundamental Thirteen: Know What You Stand For

Practical: Spend some time and really determine what politics means to you and what areas you are willing to make a difference in. Grab your same friend that you discussed your ethics categories with and have another discussion. Agree to disagree and go through the process of talking about these issues rationally and with conviction on why you stand for what you stand for. Decide if it is time for you to take action politically or get involved in a non-profit group.

Fundamental Fourteen: Know Your Personality

Practical: Take a free online personality test. Any one of them will help you discover what your personality traits are. Ask yourself what you like about your results and what you don't. Ask yourself if there is anything you would like to change and get started on it.

Fundamental Fifteen: Live Your Passion

Practical: Review the section titled, What Do I Want to Be When I Grow Up, in this chapter and spend some time asking the following three questions: What areas of life do I really enjoy? What are my skills and abilities? How can I get paid using my skills and abilities in the area of life that I really enjoy? Now, for the big-time practical. Ask yourself if what you are currently doing for work and money matches up with the answer you just came up with. If it does not, talk to your employer to set you up in a different area, or begin to set yourself up doing something you were meant to do. This practical is a biggie, but you are going to be dead someday and you probably spend most of your week working, so you might as well do something you love. Why not? You don't have to quit your day job just because you start on this quest.

CHAPTER EIGHT: FAITH AND SPIRITUALITY

Fundamental Sixteen: Cement Your Spiritual Truths

Practical: Now is the time to get your unanswered spiritual questions answered. Your relationship with your creator is too much of a source of strength to get lost in the details and questions you have carried on your shoulders for years. Decide what you believe. Spirituality is your personal belief. Decide what is going to work for you and begin to practice it. When do you think is a good time to create a relationship with your creator that can be your source of: Unconditional Love, Strength, Wisdom, Encouragement, Security, Guidance, Peace, and Understanding? Cement your spiritual truths.

CHAPTER NINE: THE PURPOSE OF LIFE

Fundamental Seventeen: The Ultimate Purpose

Practical: Ask yourself how you can show your love for God. Ask yourself how you can be your best. Ask yourself how you can help others on a regular basis. Write down on your Elevate sheet you are creating: My Purpose is to Love God, Be My Best and Help Others. Review this every morning and watch how your view changes of the world when you know that this is your ultimate purpose.

Practical: Pick a morning this weekend and go by yourself with your journal to sit somewhere you can see the sunrise. As it rises, think of everything you are grateful for in your life and tell God you love Him. Enjoy a warm cup of coffee or tea as you experience the awe of loving God.

Practical: Review what you came up with on how you can be your best. Honestly ask yourself if you are living up to your potential. If you are not, then make some decisions to do so. You are worth it. Let your light shine.

Practical: Take a drive with a friend today and look for a person on the corner holding up a sign for money. Ask them what their story is and determine for yourself if they are making an effort to help themselves productively or if they are not mentally stable. Help them with your words or money based on what you sense.

PART THREE: THE ELEVATE MINDSET— HOW TO THINK WELL

CHAPTER TEN: CHOICE AND RESPONSIBILITY

Fundamental Eighteen: Who Programmed You?

Practical: Look back at Fundamental Twelve and review what your fundamental beliefs are in each category: God, Health, Family, Wealth. Now ask yourself if what you wrote down is getting the results you want in your life. Now ask yourself where you learned that belief about that area. If it is still working for you, then great; if it is not, change it to a belief that you may not believe yet but you feel it is a good one to move toward. Update your Key Areas of Life list and review it daily.

Fundamental Nineteen: Take Advice from Winners

Practical: Look at your Key Areas of Life list again. Think of the most successful person you know in each area: God, Health, Family, Wealth. Connect with them and ask them what their fundamental beliefs are in each area. Review your list with what they said and see if you would like to change anything. Update your Key Areas of Life list and review it daily.

Fundamental Twenty: Guard Your Thoughts

Practical: Review the Winner versus Weenie Section in this chapter and take an honest assessment of which column you fall into. If you fell into the Weenie section, analyze it and ask yourself what you need to do to get over to the Winner section.

Practical: For the next three days set your phone timer to go off once an hour during your waking hours. When it goes off, write down the emotional state that you are currently experiencing. After three days, determine what your dominate emotion was for the last three days. If it is not one that is positive, ask yourself what caused it. Dig deep and determine what you need to do to change it to a positive emotion.

Practical: Put a rubber band around your wrist for three days. Every time you complain or gossip, give yourself a snap! If you snapped it even once, put the rubber band on your other wrist and do the same exercise for three days. Continue to do this until you make it three days without any complaining or gossiping.

Fundamental Twenty-One: Who Are Your Influences?

Practical: Ask yourself who you currently get advice from and ask yourself if they have the results in their life that you want in the area you are asking them for advice in. If they don't, find someone else you can get advice from.

Practical: Take an honest assessment of the five people you spend most of your time with. Ask yourself if you are all headed in the same direction. Ask yourself if you want to be like them. If they are committed to self-growth, then keep the relationship going because you will have a buddy to grow with. If they are not *and* you don't want to be like them, introduce them to self-development and get them on board. If they aren't into it, then it's time to start getting some new friends. Determine who you want to develop a friendship with and go after it.

Fundamental Twenty-Two: Reactive Versus Choosing Response

Practical: Ready to get slapped some more? Just kidding. You are going to let someone pinch you instead. Get a friend to pinch you repeatedly and steadily in the arm. Tell them to not stop no matter what unless you say the safe word, "*Elevate!*" Have them keep doing it until you begin to feel a little agitated about it. Right before you get angry decide to choose your response, take a deep breath in and say, "*Elevate! It's time to stop now.*" You are the only one who will know if you chose your response or just reacted. Keep doing it until you can honestly say that you are absolutely choosing your response. Get ready for some bruises on this one. Proceed with caution at your own risk! If you need to switch arms, do it!

Fundamental Twenty-Three: Total Responsibility

Practical: Ask yourself if there are any areas of your life that you are excelling at *and* are not excelling at. Then ask yourself what you are doing to cause that. Tell a friend what you are doing to get, or not get, what you want and how you may be getting in your own way. Tell them what you need to do to excel in those areas.

CHAPTER ELEVEN: ATTITUDE AND HAPPINESS

Fundamental Twenty-Four: Morning Affirmations

Practical: Go to www.ElevateBook.com/Bonus and download the free Elevate Affirmation poster. Put it up next to where you are going to see it every morning and begin to read this every day upon rising. Say them with emotion!

Fundamental Twenty-Five: Gratefulness

Practical: Grab a friend and write real big on a poster board the word GRATEFULNESS. Go to a crowded place, place the poster board over your head and shout out everything you are grateful for. When you are finished, hand it to a stranger and say, "You're next!" Have fun with this and commit to getting at least one other person to repeat what you just did.

Fundamental Twenty-Six: Do What You Love

Practical: Write down every activity you do that makes you feel happy. Enter into your calendar a repeating event once a month that says, "Elevate: Schedule What Makes Me Happy!" Begin to do at least once a month what makes you happy and never stop.

Fundamental Twenty-Seven: Confront

Practical: Ask yourself who you need to confront. Ask yourself who has done something that you need to discuss with them. Review the confrontation formula in this chapter under the Confrontation section and take action on it. I know this can be hard, but if you do it, you will never turn back.

CHAPTER TWELVE: CREATING CONGRUENT PROGRAMS

Fundamental Twenty-Eight: Clearing Up Any Maybes

Practical: Ask yourself if you have any items or projects that you have not yet decided on. Make the list out and get to work! Make up your mind to stop leaving those in limbo and get them done. Don't let them take up any more precious space in your brain.

CHAPTER THIRTEEN: SELF-LEADERSHIP

Fundamental Twenty-Nine: Focus

Practical: Recite the alphabet backwards from Z to A. Now have a friend yell loudly in your face and firmly tap you all over your body. Repeat the alphabet backwards until you are able to do it while the distractions are happening as good as you were able to do it without them.

Fundamental Thirty: Commitment to Excellence

Practical: Commit to picking up any pieces of trash you see at your office from now on. Every time you see a piece of trash lying outside or a small one on the floor inside, commit to excellence and pick it up. When you don't and pass it by, be committed enough to turn around and pick it up. Do this until you have developed the personality that commits to excellence in everything you do. Walk around your office or home now and pick up any trash that needs to be picked up.

Fundamental Thirty-One: Be Decisive

Practical: Make a decision on everything that is asked of you from now on. Refuse to say, "I don't care, where do you want to go?" Grab your buddy and have them ask you three questions that you need to make a decision on. Your friend can make them up if they need to. Have them offer you choices that you need to decide on.

Fundamental Thirty-Two: Perseverance

Practical: It's time to put on your running shoes because we are going for a run! Put on your gym clothes and run as far as you can until your body says quit. As soon as your body tells you to quit, commit to running another ten seconds as fast as you can, no matter what! This is definitely not easy; however, the exercise will show you that you can push through the resistance and make it farther than you would have if you weren't a person that perseveres.

Fundamental Thirty-Three: Delayed Gratification

Practical: Go out to dinner with a friend and order your favorite dessert. When you get it to your table, smell it and really create a desire for it. Set your timer for ten minutes and let it sit in front of you. When the timer goes off, take one bite of it, call the waiter over, and let them know you are finished with it. One bite, send it away, and go home knowing you are in control.

Fundamental Thirty-Four: Self-Discipline

Practical: In a previous fundamental you put up the *Elevate* affirmations poster. This is now becoming part of your routine every morning. For the next thirty days, commit to your morning affirmations and mark your calendar every day you say them. If you miss a day, then start over with a new set of thirty days.

PART FOUR: THE ELEVATE ACTION— IT'S GO TIME, BABY

CHAPTER FOURTEEN: WHAT DO I WANT?

Fundamental Thirty-Five: Goals

Practical: Get clear on your goals in the Health, Wealth, and Relationship categories. Ask yourself what you want in each category. Make it specific and measureable. Put a deadline for its completion. You read a lot about thinking big in this chapter. In each category, set a twelve-week goal. Show yourself what you can accomplish in twelve weeks!

Fundamental Thirty-Six: Five-Step Action Jackson

Practical: Go to www.ElevateBook.com/Bonus and watch the Five-Step Action Jackson video in this chapter. Show the dance to a friend until you both have the dance down.

Practical: Look at the goals you set for your Health, Wealth, and Relationships, and one at a time, put them into the Five-Step Action Jackson formula. Follow each step and fill out the formula completely for each goal. This action alone will make you feel on top of the world. These steps may require you getting some help, so if you need help, get it. The practical here is to be totally armed with your action plan for all three goals. Once you have the three goals written out in the formula, share them with the person you decided will be supporting you. Review your plan twice a day upon rising and going to bed, and you will get there!

Fundamental Thirty-Seven: Fear and Courage

Practical: Go with a friend to your grocery store and lie down on the floor and twiddle your thumbs thirty times. Make sure you do it in an area up front where people are going to walk by you or stop. If someone asks you what you are doing, tell them you are taking a break and need to rest for a minute. Before you do this, you are going to hear the Mulaheenie, big time, shout all kinds of fear into your brain. Recognize the voice, smash it, and lie down without thinking about it. Your next thought will be, "Wow, I'm on the ground doing this and conquering my fear." This practical, like the other practicals that take courage, will be some of the best memories you create from your *Elevate* experience. I know this one can be scary, but that is why it is fundamental to conquer fear and be courageous!

CHAPTER FIFTEEN: THE HABITS OF HEALTH

These practicals will be the sum of the Five Habits of Health: Avoid Toxins, Get a Wellness Chiropractic Adjustment and Massage Regularly, Eat Right, Exercise, and Practice The *Elevate* Mindset.

Fundamental Thirty-Eight: Avoid Toxins

Practical: Go through your house and start throwing out your toxins! Review the most common toxins in this chapter and get to work eliminating them. If this is too big a step for you, start with one thing on the list.

Fundamental Thirty-Nine: Get a Wellness Chiropractic Adjustment and Massage Regularly

Practical: Get a referral to a wellness chiropractor and massage therapist to have your spine, posture, and muscle balance checked for any areas that need to be corrected or improved. If you would like a referral, visit www.discoverhealthandwellness.com.

Fundamental Forty: Eat Right and Exercise

Practical: It's time to eat right and exercise. Really dive into this chapter again and firm up your plan. Begin your nutrition and exercise plan. It is time to make this a habit. The Five-Step Action Jackson will help you stay consistent. For this practical, visit your local health club and discuss your goals with a personal trainer that will be able to help you achieve what you want.

Fundamental Forty-One: The Elevate Mindset—Dealing With Stress

Practical: Review the three main points in this chapter under the Elevate Mindset section. Number one: Love God, yourself, and people. This was our first practical. Number two: Practice total responsibility. This practical was previously done in Chapter 10. Number Three: Recognize stress and deal with it. When you feel a sense of stress coming on, take a break and find out what is causing it. See if it is uncertainty, fear, or lack of preparation. Address it or accept it. Remember that everything that is happening to you is an opportunity to grow as a person.

CHAPTER SIXTEEN: THE HABITS OF WEALTH

Fundamental Forty-Two: The Origination of Money

Practical: Read the story titled Pork Chops again. Make sure you are clear and understand why money was invented. Hold up a dollar bill and ask yourself if the dollar bill you are holding is good or bad? Make sure you realize that it is a piece of paper to make our lives easier to buy things, go places, and help others.

Make sure you realize that it is good to have as much money as you can and that the amount of money you have is equal to the amount of service you give to the world. Make sure and realize that you get money by providing service and value that people want and need.

Realize that money is used to buy things you want and need, to have experiences you want to have, and to help people who cannot help themselves or are doing their best to help themselves.

Fundamental Forty-Three: Money Mindset

Practical: Review the Poverty mindset and the Wealth mindset. Discuss the principles found in this chapter with a friend.

Fundamental Forty-Four: Financial Plan

Practical: Make an appointment with a financial advisor and set up your monthly budget for your expenses to include ten percent to charity and ten percent to your savings plan. Once your savings is equivalent to three months living expenses, begin to invest. Also make sure your budget includes an extra debt payoff amount monthly. Once your plan is complete with your financial planner, make sure to have concrete dates and financial goals that you are working toward.

Fundamental Forty-Five: Carry Cash

Practical: Save up at least five hundred dollars to put in your wallet or purse and never touch it. Carry this amount with you at all times. Begin to see how this makes you feel.

Fundamental Forty-Six: Personal Financial Statement

Practical: Type out a spreadsheet of all of your assets and liabilities and calculate your net worth. Your financial planner can help you with this. Schedule to update your personal financial statement every three months. As you watch your debt go down and your savings go up, you will develop a very healthy appreciation for money.

CHAPTER SEVENTEEN: THE HABITS OF MARRIAGE

Fundamental Forty-Seven: Interview Your Spouse

Practical: If you are not married yet, read the twenty interview questions for your potential spouse in this chapter. Get clear on what you are looking for and when the opportunity arises, jump on it! If you are married, take your spouse on a date and pretend you are interviewing them for the first time. Review the twenty questions together and remind yourselves why you got married in the first place.

Fundamental Forty-Eight: Marriage Best Practices

Practical: This time have your spouse take you on a date and review the Marriage Best Practices list. Review which areas you both are doing well at and which areas need some improvement. Come away from that date with a top three to do list for each other.

Fundamental Forty-Nine: Communication Gems

Practical: Role-play with your spouse each communication gem until it feels natural. Both of you take turns and act out different situations.

Fundamental Fifty: Schedule the Five Habits

Practical: Review the Five Habits of Marriage at the end of the chapter and adopt these or choose your own. Schedule these into your calendar and do them for as long as you want a happy marriage.

CHAPTER EIGHTEEN: THE HABITS OF PARENTING

Fundamental Fifty-One: Habits to Develop Your Kids

Practical: Review these habits and really make it a point to commit to these for your children. Make sure you and your spouse are on the same page with these and get after it.

Fundamental Fifty-Two: Perform the Practicals for Kids

Practical: If you haven't started the kid practicals yet, do them.

CHAPTER NINETEEN: RITUALS AND REFLECTION

Fundamental Fifty-Three: Morning Ritual

Practical: Set a daily morning time to begin your morning ritual to consist of: attitude, reading, exercising, listening to inspirational audio, practicing your spirituality, reviewing your Be-Do-Have list, affirming what you want, and visualizing. This will become your magic time that you will greatly look forward to every morning.

Fundamental Fifty-Four: Weekly Reflection

Practical: Schedule your Weekly Reflection time for at least thirty minutes. This is your time to spend by yourself every week to make sure you are on track. You will love this time, too!

Fundamental Fifty-Five: The Gut Check

Practical: Pick an accountability partner that will go through the Gut Check steps with you at least once a quarter.

COMPLETION!!!

Congratulations! You did it! How do you feel? I would love to hear your success stories! I look forward to hearing from you!

ELEVATE PRACTICALS— CHILDREN

The following list includes practicals for raising your kids the *Elevate* way; however, as they get older, I would share with them everything that you resonated with in this book. At what age you want them to perform those lessons will be up to you.

The following categories are in order and should be followed as such. They correlate to the chapters in the book. Some will be more age specific, so skip those until appropriate. Make this time fun with your kids. Our family's ritual is to perform these lessons in a fun way once a week. These lessons will form their foundation and instill habits into their lives that will soon become subconscious ones that will serve them incredibly.

Depending on your kid's ages, you may need to get them on board with these practicals. It may take a little convincing. Here's the solution. Find out what they want. Find out what is important to them right now at this stage of their life. Once you have that information, link how doing these exercises will help them get what they want and strengthen what is important to them now. After reading this book, I know you will be able to link these exercises to anything and everything that is important to them. Be creative and you will be able to make the link.

Kids really are our future. Let's get their heads on straight now while we can still program them. Can you imagine if your parents spent thirty minutes with you a week downloading these principles into your brain? If you do not have children, pass this on to a friend that does.

Maybe you will be inspired to start an *Elevate* kids club in your local community! Be the change! Be the change! Be the change! Have fun! God Bless and Keep Smiling!

PART ONE: THE ELEVATE SELF—YOUR BEGINNING TO GREATNESS

CHAPTER ONE: LOVE

Fundamental One: Introduce Them to God

Practical: Teach them that they were created by a loving creator. He made them with all of the love in His heart. Tell them that God loves them no matter what and He teaches us to love Him, to love ourselves, and to love each other just as much as He loves us. Have them tell you how much God loves them with their arms spread as wide as they can. Have them tell you how much they love themselves. Ask them what they can do to show love to others by helping them. Go to your neighbor's house and have them do what they came up with to show love to another person.

Takeaway: When your child knows that they were created by a God that loves them and wants them to shine His love for themselves and everyone around them, it gives them an unconditional source of love that will never disappoint them and always knows what is best for them. This gives your child "the light" that will never go dark and will be recognized by others. It will help them in all areas of their life. This lesson shows them that as a human being created by God, it is their job to show others love by helping them.

Fundamental Two: Unconditional Love and Trust and Communication

Practical: Role-play with examples as you say to your child, "If you were to do something really amazing, how much would I love you? If you were to really mess up, how much would I love you? What would happen if you told me if you really messed up? What would happen if you didn't tell me and I found out later? What would happen if you really messed up and did something wrong and I never found out?"

Takeaway: Your child needs to know that you love them no matter what, unconditionally. They can come to you with any challenge they ever have. If they mess up, you still love them and are there to help them. Your children need to know they can tell you anything. It doesn't mean there won't be consequences. What it does mean is that if they tell you about something they did wrong and it warrants parental consequences, it will be a different and less severe consequence if they tell you versus you finding out without them telling you. They need to know that if you never found out, they would still know it and it would make them feel bad about themselves and that it is not okay to feel that way about yourself. The lesson here is to firmly bond your parent/child relationship with unconditional love, trust, and communication.

Your children are going to mess up and do wrong things a lot, just like you did. The important thing is to make sure they know that their choices have consequences that will affect them directly, keeping them from getting what they want out of life. It is much better to have these conversations when your child steals a pencil from school in third grade so they will feel safe to call you as a teenager when they are at a party and drink alcohol, for example.

Fundamental Three: Schedule One-On-One Time With Your Kids Weekly to do Something You Both Enjoy

Practical: Ask them what you both can do together all by yourselves for at least fifteen minutes every week. Do it now and then schedule it weekly.

Takeaway: This habit sets you both up for a lifetime of love and connection. The most important thing to young children is time with their parents. Making this time for them every week shows them that they have self-worth and are important to you. When you make them feel important by your individual time, they will gain confidence and feel important enough to make decisions that support the image they have of themselves.

CHAPTER TWO: CHARACTER

Fundamental Four: Teach Them The Big Six: Honesty, Respect, Loyalty, Faith, Courage, and Love

Practical: Make six flash cards with one Big Six character trait on each one. Go over each one before bedtime and discuss what it means and have them give you some examples of how to follow them and examples of situations that would not be following them.

Takeaway: As common as these are to you, they need to be taught to your children. When a child grows up with these fundamental character traits, they will be happier and more successful to achieve their dreams. When a child knows that they will not always follow the Big Six, but they will know when their actions are going against the Big

Six, this becomes their conscious and a huge part of their guiding light to get what they want long-term.

CHAPTER THREE: MORAL CODE

Fundamental Five: Teach Them The Bad Six: Lie, Cheat, Steal, Destroy, Mentally Harm, or Physically Abuse

Practical: Make six flash cards with one of the Bad Six traits on each one. Go over each one before bedtime along with the Good Six and discuss what it means. Have them give you some examples of situations that would fall into these categories. Make sure they understand that sometimes they might do the Bad Six, and that if they do, it is their job to let you know so you can help them get over it and make it right.

Takeaway: Once again, as obvious as these are to you, they may not be as obvious to your children. When your child knows what is right and wrong, they will make decisions based on this moral code. When a child knows that they will not always avoid the Bad Six, but will do their best every day to avoid them, they will be happier.

CHAPTER FOUR: FORGIVENESS OF SELF AND OTHERS

Fundamental Six: Teach Them to Always Forgive Themselves and Others

Practical: Observe them until you see them doing something that they know they should not be doing, like hitting their brother for example. After you handle the sibling rivalry, pull them aside and ask them the following: Do you know what you just did was wrong? How do you feel about that? Do you know that even though you just did something that was wrong, we all do things that are wrong? Do you know that forgiving yourself for what you just did means you know what you did was wrong, you still love yourself, and you are going to do your best to not do it again? Do you know that God and I still love you with all of our hearts even though you just did something that you shouldn't have? Do you think if someone did what you just did, to you, would you be able to forgive them, just like you did to yourself? Would you still be able to love them knowing you also do things like that sometimes?

Takeaway: Children need to know that they are human just like everyone else and they are going to do wrong things toward others and others are going to do wrong things toward them. Forgiveness is about knowing that we are all works in progress on the same path at different stages.

CHAPTER FIVE: SELF-ACCEPTANCE AND SEEKING APPROVAL

Fundamental Seven: Get Them in the Morning Habit of Reading Affirmations and Positive Quotes

Practical: Have them stand in front of the mirror and say, "I love myself, I love myself, I love myself!"

Takeaway: If we don't program their minds for success, no one else will. By instilling a strong, healthy love for themselves, they will be much better equipped with the strength they will need when it comes to approval of others. When they have a strong healthy love for themselves, they will not need approval from others.

CHAPTER SIX: BELIEVE IN YOURSELF

Fundamental Eight: Teach Them How Strong They Are When They Decide to Be

Practical: Take your kids to the neighborhood recreation center and have them go on the diving board even though they are scared to do it. Recognize their fear and have them repeat over and over, "I can do it! I am strong! I can do it! I can do it!"

Takeaway: This small accomplishment will spill over into every situation in their life when fear creeps in. They will be able to go back to this experience and fuel their belief in themselves.

Fundamental Nine: Give Them an Opportunity to Experience Achievement

Practical: Put your child in a local sports team that they are excited about. Every time they do their best, make sure they know how awesome they are and how they really had to believe in themselves to go for it the way they did. You can also do this for a creative school project that they did their best on and really went for it.

Takeaway: When a child experiences the sense of achievement, it reinforces the belief in themselves that they can be anything they want to be.

PART TWO: THE ELEVATE PURPOSE—WHO ARE YOU?

CHAPTER SEVEN: RECOGNIZING YOUR STRENGTHS AND PRIORITIES

Fundamental Ten: Core Values

Practical: Teach them to make decisions regarding their core values. Print out a master list of core values online and have them pick six. You can also use the Big Six if you would like. Role-play out a situation that will require them to make a decision. It needs to be relevant to them at their current age. Have them go through their list of core values and see how each value would be affected by the potential right and wrong decision. For example, you act out a scene where you are offering them the opportunity to be part of the school play. If their core values were the Big Six you would ask them; Honesty: If you say yes, will this be an honest thing to do? Respect: Would you be disrespecting anyone or anything if you decide to join the school play? Loyalty: Are you violating any other group that you belong to? Faith: Do you think that no matter how the experience turns out, it will help you grow as a person? Courage: Are you afraid to do it and is this an opportunity to be brave? Love: Is this something you really feel you would like to do? Based on their answers, ask them what their decision is.

Takeaway: People who make decisions based on their core values are not only happier because they feel good knowing they are making the right decisions for themselves and for their future, but they are also more successful in getting what they want. When your children have this tool, they can avoid getting lost in indecisiveness.

Fundamental Eleven: Key Areas of Life: God, Health, Family, Wealth

Practical: Sit down with them and go over the four most important areas in life. Make sure they have a good understanding about what each one is and how it affects everything that is important to them if one of these areas gets neglected. Of course, your key areas may be different.

Takeaway: When your child knows that each of these areas of life is integrally connected, they will keep them as priorities. Most everything they will want in their life will be easier to achieve and more fulfilling when they have a solid appreciation for their Key Areas of Life to continually focus on.

Fundamental Twelve: Strengths and Priorities

Practical: Ask them what they think they are good at. Ask them what they think they need to do better at. Continue to help them develop their strengths and areas that need improvement. Make sure they know they are a work in progress and they will be able to do some things better than others and that others will be able to do some things better than them.

As they get older, get them involved in extra-curricular activities that help bring out their strengths. When it comes time to finding out what they want to be when they grow up, make sure you guide them in the direction of an area that they love, and that matches their strengths and skill sets.

Takeaway: There will always be an opportunity within what they love to do that matches their skill set. When kids do what they are good at, they enjoy it. When a child enjoys an activity, it keeps them active. When they are active with the good stuff, it keeps them from searching for other things to do that may not be good for them. When a child knows they can pick a career path in life that they are excited about, and that there will always be opportunity doing what they love, they will be able to serve the world in the biggest possible way, using their gifts, and doing what they love.

CHAPTER EIGHT: FAITH AND SPIRITUALITY

Fundamental Thirteen: Get Your Kids Involved With a Like-Minded Spiritual Community

Practical: Take your kids to church. Introduce them to a spiritual community that you are in line with. Make sure they know what God represents and how to connect with Him. Teach them to pray and meditate. Have them begin to say everything they are grateful for every morning or evening.

Takeaway: When your child gets involved with other children that have the same spiritual values, it gives them a stronger opportunity and social connection to thrive emotionally. It teaches them what is right, how to live, and gives them social fulfillment. When a child knows they can talk to God, the answers they need in life will come to them. When they know they are "connected," it gives them the strength and peace that they will absolutely need in life. When they are grateful, it keeps them from becoming spoiled brats and/or entitled adults.

CHAPTER NINE: THE PURPOSE OF LIFE

Fundamental Fourteen: The Ultimate Purpose

Practical: Take a walk with your child and teach them why they were born. Ask them what their favorite way to love God is. Ask them what being their best means to them. Ask them why it is important to help others. Now do the activities. Love God together in the way your child expresses their love to Him. Get down on the ground and do as many push-ups as you can together, and afterwards, ask them if they did their best. If they didn't, do it again, and this time, ask them to do their best. Lastly, ask your child what project their school is asking for support on and get them involved.

Takeaway: When your child knows that their purpose here on Earth is to Love God, Be Their Best, and Help Others, they will be balanced and on purpose from day one. All decisions they will need to make based on what they want to specifically do with their life will be based on life's purpose. Every decision they will need to make as adults can run through this filter of life's purpose.

PART THREE: THE ELEVATE MINDSET— HOW TO THINK WELL

CHAPTER TEN: CHOICE AND RESPONSIBILITY

Fundamental Fifteen: Friends

Practical: Look at your child's closest friends. Find out from your child what they like about them. Ask your child if they think their current friends are good ones. If you both agree that they are, help strengthen the relationship. If they are not, ask your child if they want to be like them. If they don't, then ask them to make some new friends. Help them understand that the influence of the crowd they hang out with can influence their decisions in life. Those decisions will either support or destroy their future.

Takeaway: We all know if you hang out with dogs, you're gonna get fleas. You can't soar with eagles if you're spending too much time with turkeys. If all your friends are chickens, you're gonna get fried. Enough said.

Fundamental Sixteen: Thoughts Become Things

Practical: Ask your child to think of their favorite color and then visualize different types of cars with that color. Then ask them how many of those colored cars did they see yesterday. When they don't know, ask them to count the specific colored cars they are going to see today until they get to fifty. Teach them that what they focus on, they get.

Takeaway: When your child begins to focus on what they want, they will get so much of it that by the time they are an adult, this will become one of their biggest strengths. They will go after the opportunities that present themselves that are in alignment with what they want.

Fundamental Seventeen: Reactive Versus Choosing Response

Practical: Tickle your child until they joyfully and uncontrollably scream, "Stop!" Now this time, tell them that instead of reacting without thinking about it and screaming "stop," when they are ready for you to stop, have them take a deep breath and say, "Please stop now." Tickle them now! You can also do this lesson by observing them lose their temper with a sibling. As soon as you witness them yelling at their sibling, handle the situation and then point out that they were just reacting instead of choosing their response. Continually teach them to recognize the emotion right before they are going to react, and then take a deep breath in and choose their response.

Takeaway: When we react instead of choose our response, we lose control. This is a practical that will take many, many times to train their brains to choose their response. When your kids learn this new path of responding, they will not need to take anger management classes as adults.

Fundamental Eighteen: Total Responsibility

Practical: Ask them what they want. Whatever they want, ask them how they can earn it or get it. Once they have the answer to that, ask them if they do not get what they want, whose fault is it? Ask them if they would like your support in getting what they want and then set them up to help them achieve it.

Ask them what is most important to them in their life right now. Ask them that if they are not happy with the results they are getting in that area of life, who is responsible for that?

The next time your child says they are bored, ask them who is responsible for that and what can they do to not be bored.

Takeaway: When a child knows that their happiness is their responsibility, they will grow into happy productive adults. Of course they are dependent on us right now; however, develop their mindset now that their life is their responsibility.

Fundamental Nineteen: Choices and Consequences

Practical: Teach them that your job as their parent is to give them the tools they will need in life to get what they want and to be happy. Some of those tools are choices and consequences. Teach them that when they break the rules that are there to help them, they are making the choice to do so, and it affects them negatively. Teach them that the bad choices they make will affect their life poorly and not help them to achieve what they want to achieve.

Once they are about twelve or thirteen years old, take them and their two best friends to a teen pregnancy center, a teen juvenile hall, and a teen drug rehab center. Need I say more?

Takeaway: If you don't want a rebellious teenager, get away from the rules and punishment mode and get into the choices and consequences mode. There can still be punishment; however, make it about their choice, not about the rule. Their life is their responsibility and the sooner they realize that, the faster they will begin to make *better* choices. Your kids will develop the mindset that, "If I break this rule, I am making that choice and am willing to accept the consequence of my actions."

CHAPTER ELEVEN: ATTITUDE AND HAPPINESS

Fundamental Twenty: Morning Affirmations and Exercise

Practical: Give them a list of positive kid affirmations that you can get online and have them read one every morning followed by twenty-five jumping jacks. Check out www.ElevateBook.com/Bonus if you would like a free *Elevate* affirmations poster. Put it up in their room.

Takeaway: When we program our child's mind to be positive and happy, our child is positive and happy. People around them become positive and happy and the world becomes positive and happy.

Fundamental Twenty-One: Gratefulness

Practical: You already have them sharing what they are grateful for every morning or evening. Now help them begin to use this tool in everyday life. Have them point out ten things they are grateful for that they see and experience throughout the day. Train their hearts to be grateful.

Takeaway: Kids who learn gratefulness are happy and well balanced. Gratefulness is the key emotion that gets us back to happiness quickly.

Fundamental Twenty-Two: Do What You Love

Practical: Make a list with your child listing out all of the things, places, activities, and people that they enjoy. Make four columns: Things, Places, Activities, and People. Schedule something from the list to do every month and do one thing today. Many of the things they come up with can be combined together to enjoy it even more.

Takeaway: Kids who are clear on what things, places, activities, and people they enjoy right now will be clear on what things, places, activities, and people they enjoy as they get older. If they get in the habit of scheduling what they love now, they won't give you a blank look as an adult when you ask them what they love to do.

CHAPTER TWELVE: CREATING CONGRUENT PROGRAMS

Fundamental Twenty-Three: Clearing Up Any Confusions

Practical: Take a picnic with your child in the park and ask them if they are confused or uncertain about anything in their life. Do your best to make them certain about their questions. If you don't know the answer, find out for them. If there is no answer, let them know that we can be certain that only God knows that answer and that is okay for now. If they do not know what they are uncertain about, go over some of the categories in this chapter. Highlight the key points in this chapter under the following sections: Competitive versus Non-Competitive, Selfish versus Self-Interest, Use Your Best Judgment versus Don't Judge Others, and Quit versus Commit. Go over the key distinctions between the two and ask your child to differentiate the two to confirm understanding.

Takeaway: Kids are confused about many things. Train them now that it is good to find out what they are confused about and not let it take up empty space in their minds. Uncertainty equals insanity.

CHAPTER THIRTEEN: SELF-LEADERSHIP

Fundamental Twenty-Four: Focus

Practical: Have them read a paragraph from their favorite book and ask them some specific questions about what they just read. Now tell them that they are going to do the same thing except there are going to be distractions around them this time. Their job is to focus on the page so they can answer the questions. You are going to now introduce several distractions, engaging all of the senses one at a time. After you introduce a single distraction, have them read another paragraph and to answer your questions. After they answer the questions, add another distraction and have them do the same exercise. Continue to do this until all five distractions are happening at once. You want the distractions to incorporate all of their senses. Distractions: turn up the radio, turn on the television in front of them, turn up the fan and point it in their direction, light a scented candle, and give them a piece of gum to chew on. Once they complete this drill, take them out for some ice cream!

Takeaway: Children are pulled in a million different directions all at once these days. The stronger their ability to set up the skill set of focus now, the stronger their ability to deal with distractions in their life later. Getting what they want requires focus and it is an extremely necessary skill set.

Fundamental Twenty-Five: Commitment to Excellence

Practical: Have them clean their room. Once complete, inspect their room and tell them they did a good job; however, you know who they are inside and you know they can do an even better job. Let them know that this level of cleaning might work for some kids, but not them. Say to them, "You are a (family last name), and (family last name) commit to excellence." Have *them* point out areas of their room that they could have done even better at. Have them clean their room again, and this time, clean it committing to excellence. After final inspection, ask them how they feel about themselves after doing the task while committing to excellence.

Takeaway: Kids feel much better about themselves when they know they did their best. Once they identify *who they are* as a person, to a person that commits to excellence, it becomes part of them in everything they do. Kids who commit to excellence now carry on the habit forever.

Fundamental Twenty-Six: Decisions

Practical: Pick a weekend day that is all about a family day. Tell your child that it is their job today to make the decisions. Give them multiple choices to choose from all day. Would you like eggs and fruit, or turkey bacon and a smoothie for breakfast? Would you like to play football or soccer? Would you like to have lunch at XYZ or ZYX?

Takeaway: Children are used to having decisions made for them. Empower them now with the ability to make a decision. Decisive kids become decisive adults.

Fundamental Twenty-Seven: Perseverance

Practical: Tell them that you both are going to do three hundred jumping jacks at the same time. The number will change based on the age; make it difficult but not impossible. Tell them that no matter what, they are not allowed to quit when they feel like quitting. Tell them that as soon as their body tells them to quit and they start to get tired, they *must* tell you when this happens while they *continue* to do the jumping jacks. As soon as they tell you this feeling is happening, you shout, "Okay, do not listen to your body right now! Let's do ten more! Do not stop! You are a person that pushes past the pain, pushes through the resistance! Keep going! Five more! Never give up! Time!" Your goal is to push them way past their original stopping point. Teach them to never give up and that there are only challenges and solutions in life, not problems.

Takeaway: Your kids will now know the difference between their body telling them to quit and their mind telling them to keep going. This lesson teaches them to never give up and to embrace challenges to make them stronger.

Fundamental Twenty-Eight: Delayed Gratification

Practical: Have your child sit at the kitchen table and put a marshmallow in front of them. Tell your kids that they can have a marshmallow right now or three marshmallows in ten minutes. Ask them to decide. Depending on their response, keep increasing the number of marshmallows in ten minutes until they decide to wait.

Takeaway: This exercise shows your child that good things come to those who are patient enough to wait for what they want. This discipline will carry over to many of their decisions and choices in life. It will teach them that when they know what they want, they can wait to have even more of it.

Fundamental Twenty-Nine: Self-Discipline

Practical: Have them mark their calendar for the next thirty days if they complete their morning affirmations and jumping jack ritual.

Takeaway: One of the biggest struggles adults have is sticking to a plan to get them what they want. Break this cycle for your child. As you support them in completing this fundamental, shower them with your love and encouragement, letting them know how proud you are of them completing their self-discipline project!

PART FOUR: THE ELEVATE ACTION—IT'S GO TIME, BABY

CHAPTER FOURTEEN: WHAT DO I WANT?

Fundamental Thirty: Goals

Practical: Set your child up with a goal notepad and have them write down what they want. Teach them that they can be, do, and have anything they set their mind to. Tell them if they continue to focus on their goal, they may reach challenges and may need to change their approach, but continue to persevere and go after what they have listed until they get it.

Fundamental Thirty-One: Five-Step Action Jackson

Practical: Take them to www.ElevateBook.com/Bonus and teach them the Five-Step Action Jackson dance. Have fun with them while you both do the dance together. Now open up their goal notebook and ask them by when they want to achieve their goal. Ask them what it will mean to them when they achieve it. Ask them how they will feel and what will happen if they don't. Ask them how they plan on achieving it. Ask them to include reading this goal every morning along with their affirmations. Ask them how you can support them in achieving their goal and how they can help a friend or family member who is also going after their goal. Tie all of these questions back to the dance. This may be your child's first attempt at going after what they want in life. Be the disciplined parent who supports them to show them that they *can* have what they want.

Takeaway: When kids learn that there is a formula to getting what they want, they will be filled with self-responsibility and empowerment to know that anything they set their mind to is possible. When they learn how to go after their goals systematically, they will achieve magnificent accomplishments.

Fundamental Thirty-Two: Fear and Courage

Practical: Ask them what they are afraid of. Find out what makes them scared. Ask them why. Once you have determined what they are afraid of and why, teach them about a Mulaheenie and what his job is in their minds. (See Chapter 14, section Fear and Courage) Ask them how they would like to destroy the Mulaheenie in their minds, golf club, kick, etc. Now practice with them mentally destroying the Mulaheenie with the method of their choice and instantly doing five jumping jacks as fast as they can. Now ask them how that felt. You are teaching them to recognize the voice of fear and to attack it and take action right away. Now tell them you are going to do it for real. Set up the situation, or if needed, the next time they are afraid of what you both discussed, perform this exercise. Instead of five jumping jacks, do the action they are afraid to do. This may take several attempts. Do not stop this practical until they learn to recognize the voice of fear and take action anyway. Once they do take action on what they are afraid to do, shower them with massive, massive, massive praise. Make this celebration huge!

Takeaway: That Mulaheenie puts up a strong fight at first and then he is instantly a coward after action. Kids who learn to not be afraid of the dark, for example, turn into adults who are not afraid to go after what they want.

CHAPTER FIFTEEN: THE HABITS OF HEALTH

These practicals will be the sum of the Five Habits of Health: Avoid Toxins, Get a Wellness Chiropractic Adjustment and Massage, Eat Right, Exercise, and Practice the Elevate Mindset.

Fundamental Thirty-Three: Avoid Toxins

Practical: Teach them about common toxins listed in Chapter 15 and why they should be avoided. Show examples in your home or at the store of common toxins that should be avoided most of the time. Go through your house together and start throwing things out. If this is too big of a step for you, start with one thing on the list and let them know your household is going to begin this process starting today. Teach them that those chemicals, when taken on a regular basis, will hurt them and not allow them to go after what they want in life.

Takeaway: Your children are never too young to know what chemicals are and how toxic they are to their bodies and their future. Don't be afraid to teach them about cancer. Folks, one out of three Americans are developing it! This lesson on toxins will easily equate to lessons on avoiding drugs as they get older, and it will give them a sense of appreciation for their miraculous body.

Fundamental Thirty-Four: Get a Chiropractic Wellness Evaluation

Practical: Get a referral to a wellness chiropractor that takes care of children to have their spines checked for any areas that need to be corrected. If you would like a referral, visit:

www.discoverhealthandwellness.com.

Takeaway: Your child's spine is their vehicle for life. If the structure is not correct, their nervous system will get pressure and tension on it, which reduces the function of their body.

Fundamental Thirty-Five: Eat Right and Exercise

Practical: This one starts with you. Every day let them see you exercise, even if it is only your ten jumping jacks in the morning after your affirmations. Do this exercise together. Get them in the morning habit of exercising and eating right by your example.

Have a fun five question quiz at every meal, comparing bad food to good food. Whoever gets all five questions right, gets a special bonus. "Is fried chicken or grilled chicken better for you? Is it better to drink soda or water at lunch? Which is better for you, white bread or whole grain? True or false: It is important to have a protein or healthy fat anytime you eat a carbohydrate. Name five healthy carbohydrates. Name five healthy proteins. Name five healthy fats....."

Takeaway: The best example a child has in the health category is by watching your habits and by eating what you feed them. If you exercise and eat right so will your kids. Don't let them go through life fat and unhealthy. That is not fair to do to your child. It is not good for their self-esteem and it is not good for them physically. This is where you must buck up and be part of the solution. You wouldn't have made it this far in the book if you didn't feel the same.

Fundamental Thirty-Six: The Elevate Mindset—Dealing with Stress

Practical: Teach them the three main points in Chapter 15 under the section: Elevate Mindset. Number one: Love God, themselves, and people. This was our first practical. Number two: Practice total responsibility. This practical was previously done in Chapter 10. Number Three: Recognize stress and deal with it. When you see a sense of stress in your child, take a break and find out what is causing it. See if it is uncertainty, fear, or lack of preparation. Address it or accept it. Teach them that everything that is happening to them is an opportunity to grow as a person.

Takeaway: These three principles as they relate to stress and your child's health will wipe out most areas of stress for your child. Stress is a killer, so let's set them up to conquer it. Make sure they know that too much stress is unhealthy and it is considered a bad thing for their health now and in the future.

CHAPTER SIXTEEN: THE HABITS OF WEALTH

Fundamental Thirty-Seven: Pork Chops

Practical: Read them the story of Pork Chops in Chapter 16 so they can understand where money came from. Discuss the story and make sure they understand why money was invented. Hold up a dollar bill and ask them if the dollar bill you are holding is good or bad? Take them back to the Pork Chops story and explain to them that it is neither good or bad, it is a piece of paper to make our lives easier to buy things, go places, and help others with.

Teach them that it is good to have as much money as they can and that the amount of money they have is equal to the amount of service they give to the world. Give them some business examples. "If you made a healthy donut that a million people loved, and they paid you a million dollars for the recipe, would that be a good way to make money? What are some other ways to make money?" Make sure they know that they get money by providing service that people want and need. They get money by helping people get what they need and want.

Teach them that money is used to buy things they want and need, to have experiences they want to have, and to help people who cannot help themselves or are doing their best to help themselves. After this explanation, ask them if they think it is good to have a lot of money. Next, ask them which is more important, money or people. Make sure they know that they are both important and they should both be treated with respect.

Takeaway: Your kids will come away from this conversation having a healthy respect and appreciation for money. They will be driven to help others and get paid for it.

Fundamental Thirty-Eight: Daily Communication Regarding Money

Practical: Teach them that Poverty means no money and Wealth means money. Review the Poverty Mindsets versus Wealth Mindsets section in Chapter 16. Go through each communication style that is age appropriate and make sure they are able to distinguish the difference between both mindsets.

Takeaway: When your child begins to recognize the difference between poverty communication and wealth communication, they will be able to point it out and choose wealth communication. When they talk in the Wealth mindset, they will set themselves up to get it.

Fundamental Thirty-Nine: Business 101

Practical: Ask them how they would like to make money now. Ask them what kind of business they would like to set up. This could be anything from a concert or magic show for the family, to selling us their paintings, to setting up a lemonade stand. Get them in the habit now of knowing that if they want money, they need to provide value to others and earn it.

Takeaway: If your child learns how to make money now, they will make money their entire lives. If they learn how to provide service and value to the world now, imagine what they will be doing for our world in ten to fifteen years!

Fundamental Forty: Payday

Practical: Give them a weekly payday with bonuses for completing their chores. Do not call it an allowance. Make sure they know it is earned and when they complete all of the chores on their list with no input from "management" they get an extra financial bonus for a job well done.

Takeaway: Children who learn to do a good job now and learn that when they do a good job, they get more money, make more money at every job or business they create. This not only gives them a better understanding of responsibility but also a healthy respect for money.

Fundamental Forty-One: Bank Accounts

Practical: Set them up with three containers for their bank accounts in the following order: Giving Account, Savings Account, and Spending Account. Based on their age, this can be done in their room or you can actually take them to the bank every week and help them make their deposits. At every payday, give them correct change and tell them to put a portion of it in their three accounts. Ideally, you put ten percent in the Giving, ten percent in the Savings, and let them put eighty percent in their Spending account. Divide their payday into ten equal parts so they can begin to understand what ten percent looks like. As they begin to make money on their own entrepreneurial projects, have them apply what they make each day to these accounts as well.

Takeaway: When your child learns to live on eighty percent of what they make, it becomes a part of them. When it comes time for them to have a job or start their own business, it will be an easy transition to set up automatic debit accounts for their Giving and Savings accounts.

CHAPTER SEVENTEEN: THE HABITS OF MARRIAGE

Fundamental Forty-Two: The Example of Marriage

Practical: If you are married, ask your kids how they see each parent showing love to the other one. Tell them that someday they will find someone to love and get married to and this person should be just as special and awesome as they are. Tell them that someday after college, they will find someone that they will want to spend the rest of their life with and when they do, they will be able to get married.

Takeaway: Kids learn how to love their future spouse based on how you show your love to your spouse. Kids learn how they will want to be treated by their future spouse based on how you and your spouse treat each other.

CHAPTER EIGHTEEN: THE HABITS OF PARENTING

Fundamental Forty-Three: Role Reversal

Practical: For twenty minutes have your kids pretend they are the parent and you pretend you are them. Act out certain areas that are great and areas that are challenging. For example, act out your morning breakfast together; ask them to turn off the video games or television, getting off to school, or getting ready for school.

Takeaway: This one, when played seriously, can be fun and very revealing. Kids will show you exactly how you are portrayed to them and they will see by your acting how they act toward you. It will help you understand how you act with them and it will help them understand how they act with you. This one is a game changer if you have challenges in getting them to do what you want them to do.

CHAPTER NINETEEN: RITUALS AND REFLECTION

Fundamental Forty-Four: Monitor Your Life

Practical: Ask your child how well the main four areas of their life are going: God, Health, Family, and Wealth. Perform this ritual of reflection once a week. Dinnertime works well. "On a scale of one to ten, how well is your relationship with God this week? What is keeping it from a ten? On a scale of one to ten, how well is your health plan going? What can you do next week to make it a ten? On a scale of one to ten, how are things going with us and your siblings? What can we do better together to bring that back up next week? On a scale of one to ten, how are your three accounts coming along? How can you bump those up next week?"

Takeaway: Creating this ritual of reflection once a week will give your child the habit of always wanting the most out of life and not settling for less. It will give them a time weekly where they can be open, honest, and very communicative with you. This time once a week will become one of the best tools to keep your family together and your kids headed in the right direction.

COMPLETION!!!

Congratulations! You are officially the best parent in the world! How did you do? How do you feel? I want to hear your success story! I look forward to hearing from you!

Elevate

References

The sources are listed numerically as they appear in this book.

1: American Foundation for Suicide Prevention (afsp.org)

2: Mayo Clinic March 2011

3: Morbidity and Mortality Weekly Report, Center for Disease Control 2007; 56 (05):93-96

4: Dr. David Healy, RxISK.org

5: Dr. Joseph Mercola. Why are drug companies targeting your children as customers?

6: Maggie Fox, Senior Writer, NBC News. We're unhealthier than everyone else—and it's our own fault.

7: TGCM.org

8: Hugs help kids brain—Washington University Study 2013

9: Shawn Achor. The Happiness Advantage

10: Designsforhealth.com

11: Dr. Ronald Pero, PhD, Chief of Cancer Prevention Research at NY's PMI

12: Romney paid 14.1% tax rate in 2011 CBS.com 9-21-12

13: Jennifer Baker of the Forest Institute of Professional Psychology

Elevate

Special Acknowledgments

The following acknowledgments are dedications to my professional giants that have allowed me to stand on their shoulders and make my difference to the world. You all are my heroes, and I will be forever grateful for the wealth of knowledge you have taught me. The following giants are considered my "big" boys and are listed in order of when they were introduced to my life.

Tony Robbins: Tony, although I have never met you in person, no one is able to light me up like you can. I have studied your enormous body of work for over twenty years now. I don't think you have made an audio program that I have not listened to. Thank you for having such a heart for people and such drive to inspire the millions! You, my man, are amazing! (Tonyrobbins.com)

Brian Tracy: Brian, I saw you speak for the first time over ten years ago! I bought everything you were selling, including: *The Psychology of Achievement, Master Your Time, The Psychology of Selling,* and *The Science of Self Confidence.* Your recordings shaped me into the leader I have become. Your book, *Eat That Frog* cured any procrastination I was dealing with. Thanks, Brian, your words of wisdom have allowed me to touch and transform the lives of many. You are one of my first mentors and I will always be grateful. (Briantracy.com)

Tom Cruise: I know it is a little strange that I am acknowledging you, but I have to say, the characters in your movies were made for me! I'm serious. You have inspired me for years. From *Top Gun* and *Risky Business*, to *Cocktail, Days of Thunder, The Last Samurai*, and *Jerry* Mah-fkn *Maguire*, you inspire me man! I know the media has a lot to say about you, and regardless of that, you are a courageous, convicted human being that is not afraid to be who you are.

Dr. Steve Hays: Steve, I spent the first four years of my career going to all of your seminars, and the knowledge I gained from those initial years has served me during my entire chiropractic career. Thank you, Steve! You taught me all about business and efficiency! I will always be one of your wonder boys! You gave me my first taste of success, and the memories I have with your group are cherished. (Pinnaclemanagment.net)

PSI seminars: My wife and I spent a week up in the California hills with PSI! Your seminars were life changers. I was not the same when I left. You opened my eyes. Your basic seminar is a game changer. Thank you! (Psiseminars.com)

Dr. Patrick Gentempo: Through your old *On Purpose* audios and many seminars, you made me bulletproof, Patrick. The hours upon hours of research and philosophy that you put together in such a simple format still amazes me. You took self-responsibility to a new level for me. Thank you for finally convicting me to know that if I am not part of the solution, I am part of the problem. I will always be the guy that still has the offer on the table to take you to the best Italian restaurant in Denver! (Patrickgentempo.com)

Karen Van Cleve: Karen, you have been my life success coach for over ten years! I cherish our calls and the perspective that you always help me see. Thank you for being my sounding board through all of the difficult decisions and exciting dreams that we have conquered together! (Karenvancleve.com)

Dr. Ben Lerner: Ben, you showed me what fierce passion looks like in action. You inspired me over and over to make a difference in my community, my town, my world. You will always be one of my greatest chiropractic heroes of all time. You taught me all about volume and purpose. You are a mighty man, Ben, and I thank you from the bottom of my heart for igniting my purpose. (Maximizedliving.com)

Darren Hardy: Darren, I devour your magazine every month. When it arrives in my mailbox, I am like a kid in a candy store. Your publication keeps me juiced and even inspired my wife to start the Success for Teens program at our son's school. I hope to meet you in person soon. You are a mega giant! (Success.com)

Dr. David Singer: David, you are one of the originals, my friend. You taught me about marketing, communication, and management. You are a genius. The courses I took through your organizations gave me the tools to love expansion. Thank you for introducing me to Hubbard Executive Management. The skills I learned have helped me succeed in business and in life. (Davidsingerenterprises.com)

Jon Butcher: Jon, you gave me my Lifebook, man! What an amazing tool you have created. I got really clear on all the areas of my life because of you. I love the monthly online service and so much more about the community you have created. Your work is just getting started, and I am grateful to be part of your expanding community. I look forward to traveling distant lands with you! (Mylifebook.com)

Brian Johnson: Brian, your philosophical wisdom is unmatched. You and I spend a lot of time together and I have never met you! Thank you for following your heart's desire and producing such incredible book reviews. Your audios are much more than book reviews. I love how you make ancient wisdom so relevant. Dig it! (Entheos.com/philosophersnotes)

Michael Noel: Michael, you introduced me to the emergent faith. Oh my God! Literally! You helped me get back to my faith with passion, brother! You guided me to the answers I had been seeking for years. Thank you for introducing me to the author, Brian McLaren, and thank you for introducing me to your church. You are God's hands and feet, my friend. (Thejourneychurch.com)

MORE ACKNOWLEDGEMENTS

These additional acknowledgments are authors that have impacted me greatly, and I will forever be thankful for all of the hours I have read your material and listened to your audios. I have been impacted by many more, and I apologize in advance if I neglected to include any in this list. Although some of you have left us, your work will live forever. You are all my giants, and your work has greatly impacted *Elevate*. Thank you to these additional warriors, listed here in alphabetical order.

Shawn Achor, Mitch Albom, Robert Allen, Fred Barge, Rob Bell, Nathanial Branden, Joseph Campbell, Jack Canfield, Dale Carnegie, Gary Chapman, James Chestnut, Alan Cohen, Stephen Covey, John Demartini, Wayne Dyer, John Eldridge, Tim Ferriss, Michael Gerber, Malcom Gladwell, John Gray, Bob Harrison, Glenn Hawthorne, Napoleon Hill, L. Ron Hubbard, Mike Jones, Robert Kiyosaki, Lazz Laszlo, Greg Loman, Tamara Lowe, Paul Martin, Abraham Maslow, John Maxwell, Brian McLaren, Joseph Mercola, CJ Mertz, Earl Nightingale, Dennis Nikitow, Tim O'Shea, Joel Osteen, BJ Palmer, Sam Parker, Jim Peterson, Norman Vincent Peale, Bill Phillips, Paul Zane Pilzer, Eric Plasker, Nido Qubein, Dave Ramsey, Ayn Rand, Jim Rohn, Rob Schiffman, David Schwartz, Martin Seligman, Robin Sharma, Jim Sigafoose, Sylvester Stallone, Lee Strobel, Brad Sugars, Marshall Sylver, Kevin Trudeau, Donald Trump, Denis Waitley, Charles Ward, Mike Ware, Chris Widener, John Wooden, and Zig Ziglar.

About the Author

Dr. Keppen Laszlo

As Founder and Executive Director of one of the largest groups of wellness centers in the state of Colorado, Discover Health and Wellness, Dr. Keppen Laszlo and his team of doctors have helped thousands of people live their full potential. He developed the non-profit organization, The Elevate Foundation, and he has a strong compassion for helping others step into their greatness. Dr. Laszlo is a contributor to the NY Times best-selling book, *Body by God* and *One Minute Wellness*. While continuing to tackle the rewards and challenges in his professional life, he loves spending his time with his beautiful wife of twelve years and their two fabulous boys.

Elevate

Made in the USA
Columbia, SC
08 September 2018